Grammar Rules!

Tanya Gibb

Australian Curriculum Edition

Name: ______________________________

Class: ______________________________

Grammar Rules! Student Book 3
Australian Curriculum Edition
ISBN: 978 0 6550 9251 3

Designer and typesetter: Trish Hayes
Illustrator: Stephen Michael King
Series editor: Marie James
Indigenous consultant: Al Fricker

Acknowledgement of Country
Matilda Education Australia acknowledges all Aboriginal and Torres Strait Islander Traditional Custodians of Country and recognises their continuing connection to land, sea, culture, and community. We pay our respects to Elders past and present.

This edition published in 2024 by **Matilda Education Australia**, an imprint of Meanwhile Education Pty
PO Box 118, Burwood, Victoria, Australia 3125
T: 1300 277 235
E: customersupport@matildaed.com.au
W: www.matildaeducation.com.au

First edition published in 2008 by Macmillan Science and Education Australia Pty Ltd

Publication data
Author: Tanya Gibb
Title: *Grammar Rules! Student Book 3*
Australian Curriculum Edition
ISBN: 978 0 6550 9251 3

A catalogue record for this book is available from the National Library of Australia

Printed in China by Central
Jun-2025

CONTENTS

NOTE TO TEACHERS AND PARENTS

Grammar Rules!

Grammar Rules! comprehensively addresses the interrelated strands of Language, Literature and Literacy in the **Australian Curriculum English V9**, 2022. The *Grammar Rules!* series supports students' development of knowledge, understanding and skills in reading, viewing, speaking, writing and creating texts.

The **Australian Curriculum English** recognises that learning in English is recursive and cumulative, so each book in the *Grammar Rules!* series is designed to build on concepts covered previously and for an expanding range of audiences and purposes.

Grammar Rules! provides a conceptually sound scope and sequence of context-based activities that support teaching and learning in English. Although the title for the series is *Grammar Rules!*, the series in not just about grammar. Each unit of work in the series begins at the level of the whole text by identifying purpose and audience for the model text, providing teaching opportunities to activate students' background knowledge of the topic or the text type, and then supporting students in reading comprehension. The texts provided can be used for discussion of text forms and features and sentence structures, as well as for vocabulary expansion. The texts can also be used as models for students to use when creating their own written, spoken or multimodal texts. The texts included in *Grammar Rules!* cover a variety of informative, imaginative and persuasive texts and hybrid texts that use elements of different types of texts.

Grammar Rules! also teaches the conventions of punctuation and some aspects of spelling, such as prefixes, suffixes, apostrophes and homophones, and literary elements such as onomatopoeia, simile and idiom, as well as character, setting and plot in narratives. *Grammar Rules!* comprehensively supports the aim of the **Australian Curriculum English V9** to 'help students learn to analyse, understand, communicate and build relationships with others and the world around them. It helps create confident communicators, imaginative and critical thinkers, and informed citizens.'

Student Book 3

Units of work

Student Book 3 contains 35 weekly units of work presented in a conceptually sound scope and sequence. The intention is for students to work through the units in the sequence in which they are presented. See the **Scope and Sequence Chart** on pages 6–7 for more information. There are regular Revision Units that can be used for consolidation or assessment purposes.

The sample texts in *Student Book 3* are not tied to content across any other subject area but are generally based on the theme of discoveries and inventions. This allows teachers and students to focus on the way language is structured in the different types of texts according to purpose and audience. Students can then use this knowledge to critically evaluate, respond to and create texts in other learning areas.

Icons

Encourages students to create texts of their own to demonstrate their understanding of the text structures and features taught in the unit. These activities focus on written language; however, many also provide opportunities for using spoken language to engage with others, make presentations and develop skills in using ICT.

Highlights useful grammatical rules and concepts. The rule is always introduced the first time students need it to complete an activity.

Tells students that a special hint is provided for an activity. It might be a tip about language features or a reminder to look at a rule in a previous unit.

Grammar Rules! Glossary

A valuable glossary is provided at the end of *Student Book 3*. Teachers and students can use this as a reference for terminology and rules introduced in *Student Book 3*. Page references are also given for the point in the book where the rule or tip was first introduced so that students can go back to that unit if they need more information or further revision of the concept.

Grammar Rules! Student Book 3 (ISBN 9780655092513) © Tanya Gibb

Pull-Out Writing Log

At the centre of *Student Book 3* is a practical pull-out Writing Log so that students can keep track of the texts they have created or attempted to create. The Writing Log also includes a handy reminder of the writing process, as well as a checklist of types of texts for students to try.

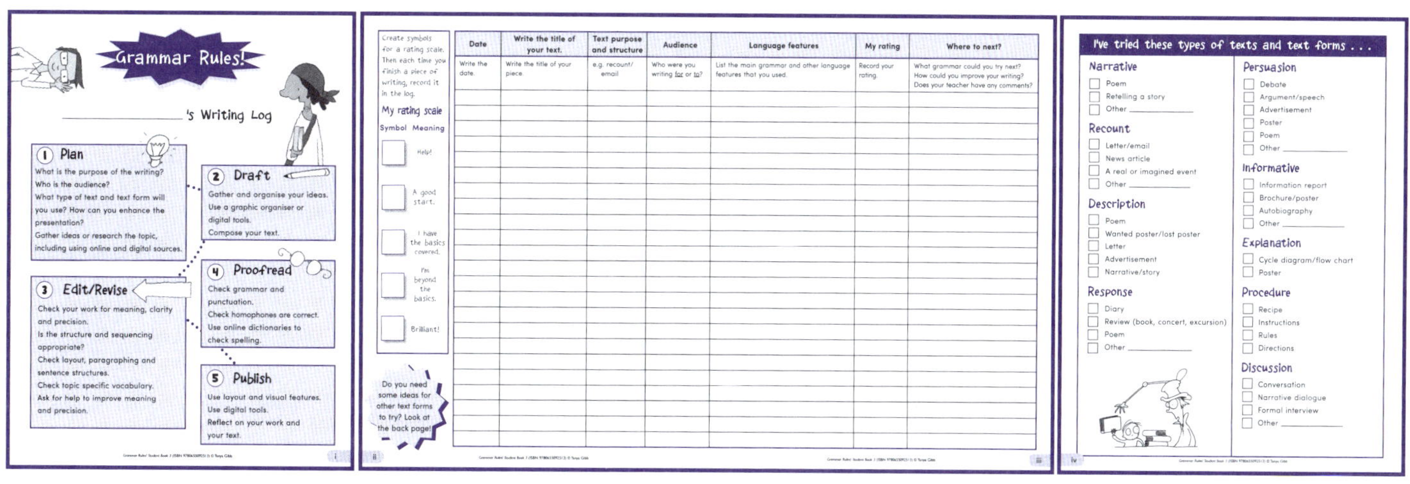

Unit at a Glance

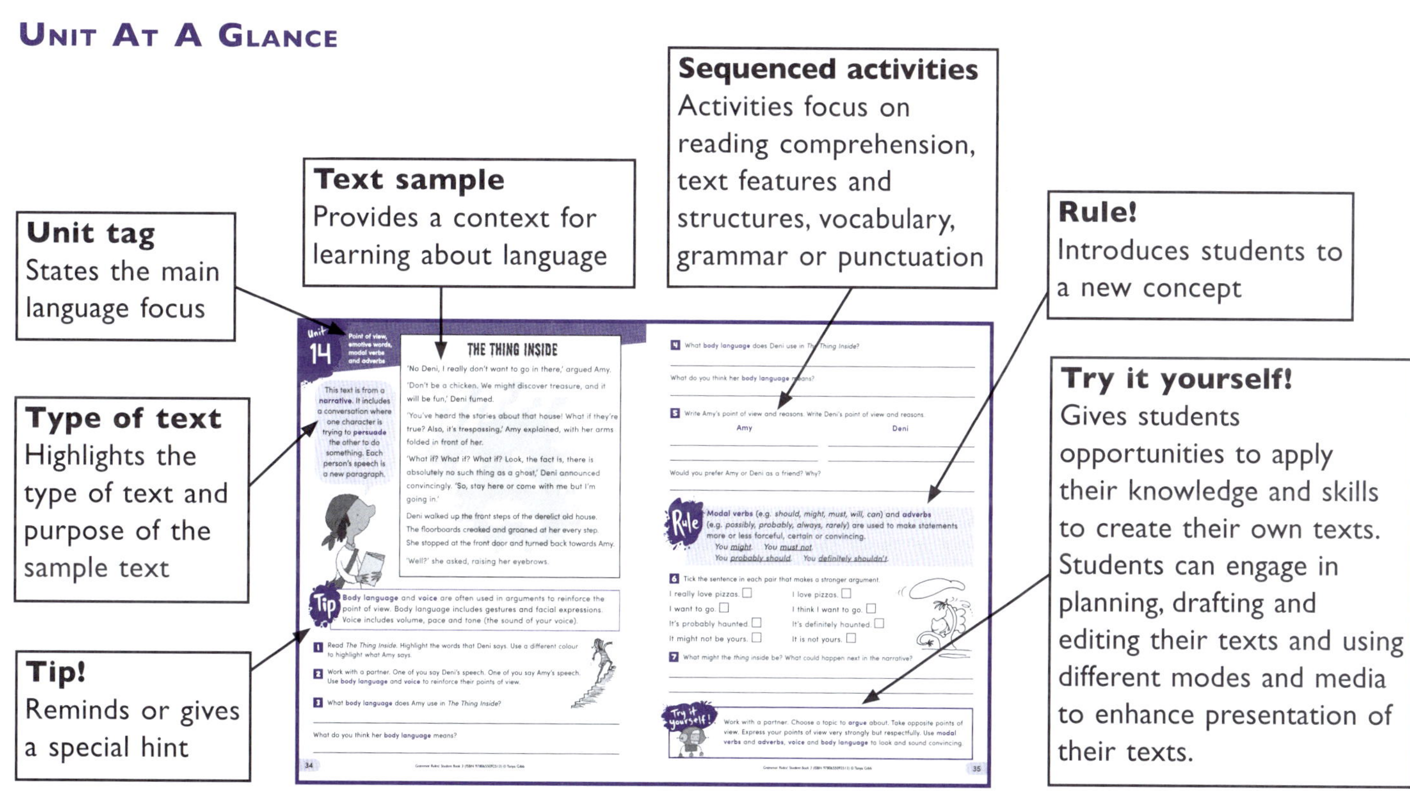

Grammar Rules! Teacher Resource Book 3–6

Full teacher support for *Student Book 3* is provided by *Grammar Rules! Teacher Resource Book 3–6*.

Here you will find valuable background information about teaching English along with practical resources, such as:

- strategies for teaching text structures and features
- teaching tips for every unit in *Student Book 3*
- answers for every unit in *Student Book 3*
- grammar and punctuation wall charts
- literacy games and activities
- assessment strategies.

Scope and Sequence

This scope and sequence chart is based on the requirements of the Australian Curriculum English.

Unit	Unit name Type of text	Purpose of text	Clauses, sentences, conjunctions	Nouns, noun groups, pronouns, adjectives	Verbs and verb groups	Adverbs and prepositional phrases, connectives	Elements of language
1	**Museum Visit** Personal recount	to retell events to respond		proper and common nouns	doing verbs, past tense		
2	**My Grandparents** Response	to inform to describe	clauses, simple sentences	adjectives, proper and common nouns			definitions, sentence boundary punctuation
3	**Dear Nana and Pop** Email	to respond	sentences, statements, questions, exclamations	personal pronouns	thinking and feeling verbs		sentence boundary punctuation
4	**The Case of the Missing Robots** Narrative	to entertain		personal pronouns, noun groups, articles, adjectives			character, setting, mystery genre
5	**Inventing Potato Chips** Film review	to respond to persuade			saying verbs, thinking verbs		opinions
6	REVISION						
7	**My Special Place** Poem	to respond to describe		noun groups, adjectives		prepositional phrases that tell where	
8	**Use Less Plastic!** Speech Argument	to persuade to argue a point of view		possessive apostrophes		prepositional phrases – where	main idea, apostrophes for contractions, opinion and reasons
9	**Penicillin** Information report	to inform	questions and statements		relating (being) verbs	adverbs/ phrases for time	sequencing events in time
10	**Molly's Discovery** Narrative	to entertain	independent clauses, compound sentences, conjunctions	singular and plural nouns	subject-verb agreement		character, setting, suffixes for plurals
11	**Search for the Lost Valley** Narrative	to entertain	exclamations	adjectives		adverbs that tell how	onomatopoeia, character, setting, evaluative language
12	REVISION						
13	**Trampolines** Discussion Conversation	to share opinions	quoted speech, questions and statements	adjectives	saying verbs	adverbs	opinions, evaluative language
14	**The Thing Inside** Narrative Discussion	to argue a point of view			modal verbs, saying verbs	modal adverbs	body language, voice, characters' dialogue
15	**Jane Goodall** Biography	to inform	sentences	possessive pronouns			word families, commas in a list and for quoted speech
16	**Wiz Bang 3000 Kitchen Hand!** Advertisement	to persuade	commands	personal pronouns	modal verbs	modal adverbs	emotive words
17	**Bush Tucker** Information report	to inform to respond to describe		noun groups, articles, adjectives that compare			
18	REVISION						

Grammar Rules! Student Book 3 (ISBN 9780655092513) © Tanya Gibb

Unit	Unit name Type of text	Purpose of text	Clauses, sentences, conjunctions	Nouns, noun groups, pronouns, adjectives	Verbs and verb groups	Adverbs and prepositional phrases, connectives	Elements of language
19	**Haiku** Information report	to inform to describe		adjectives		prepositional phrases	imagery, idiom, simile
20	**Recycle!** Speech Argument	to persuade	sentences			connectives	evaluative language, fact/opinion
21	**Professor Snodgrass Fails Again** Narrative – comic strip	to entertain	quoted speech				speech balloons, stereotypes, character
22	**Dinosaur Found at Local School** News report	to inform to report newsworthy events	quoted speech	adjectives, abstract and concrete nouns	modal verbs	adverbs	emotive words, synonyms, sensationalism
23	**The Discovery** Narrative	to entertain		adjectives	verbs, past, present and future tense	prepositional phrases	story character, judging a character
24	REVISION						
25	**The Best New Invention** Discussion – conversation	to persuade	conjunctions		modal verbs	modal adverbs	quotation marks, paragraphs
26	**Creation Stories** Information report	to inform		noun groups, adjectives – describing and number/quantity			prefixes, suffixes, punctuation
27	**Warts, Festers and Carbuncle Remover** Recipe	to inform to instruct	commands	adjectives	doing verbs	adverbs	definitions
28	**How the Alarm Bed Works** Explanation	to explain to inform	conjunctions		verb groups	adverbs	sequencing information
29	**How to Use the Drolley (or Dog Trolley)** Instructions	to instruct to inform	sentences, clauses, commands	noun groups, adjectives			logical order
30	REVISION						
31	**My Home** Poem	to respond to inform to persuade		personal pronouns, collective nouns			main idea, point of view, narrator
32	**Can We Negotiate?** Discussion Conversation	to present opinions to persuade	sentences – statements, questions, commands, exclamations		saying verbs		antonyms, punctuation, point of view
33	**Clever Inventions** Information report	to inform to persuade	personal pronouns, abstract nouns		modal verbs, verb groups		punctuation
34	**The Invention of Money** Information report	to inform		personal pronouns, noun groups			homophones, commas in lists
35	REVISION						

Unit 1

Nouns, doing verbs, tense

Museum Visit

On the weekend, Mum took me to the National Museum of Australia in Canberra.

We saw lots of interesting exhibits and displays. My favourite was the Aboriginal language game. I had to match words in the Guugu Yimithirr language with words listed by James Cook's crew on *Endeavour* in 1770. I found out that 'kangaroo' is a Guugu Yimithirr word.

We ate lunch beside Lake Burley Griffin and then we saw Paddle Steamer *Enterprise*. It is one of the oldest working paddle steamers in the world.

I had a great day.

Rule

Nouns name people, places, animals and things, including ideas.
Common nouns: *teachers* *museum* *cockatoo* *book* *peace*
Proper nouns are particular names. They begin with a capital letter.
First Nations Australians *Hobart* *Tasmanian devil* *Monday*

1 Read *Museum Visit*. Write six **common nouns** used in *Museum Visit*.

____

2 Write six **proper nouns** used in *Museum Visit*.

____

Rule

Book and text titles and names of organisations begin with a capital letter.
'The Emu Who Ran Through the Sky' by Helen Milroy, published by Magabala Books.

3 Write the title of your favourite book or television show. Use capital letters.

____

Grammar Rules! Student Book 3 (ISBN 9780655092513) © Tanya Gibb

4 Underline six **nouns** for people, places, animals or things.

We parked our car under a tree.

We watched a film about bees.

We sat at a table to eat.

Many people visit the museum.

5 Circle the **noun** in each row.

dog	skipped	ate	played
visited	drove	saw	cat
stopped	bird	climbed	watched
jumped	tickled	swan	said
talked	sang	wiggled	wombat

Verbs tell what is happening in a clause. Verbs anchor events in time. This is called **tense**. Past tense verbs show that activities happened in the past.

Past tense doing verbs: *jumped ran made wrote ate had eaten*

6 Underline a **doing verb** in each sentence.

We ate lunch.

Mum drove the car.

We walked beside the lake.

I built a robot.

We arrived at 10 o'clock.

7 Write the **past tense** form for each **doing verb**.

skip ______________

break ______________

see ______________

know ______________

teach ______________

8 Choose a **doing verb** from the box to complete each sentence.

visited	worked	slept	swam

We ______________ the museum.

Ducks ______________ on the lake.

I ______________ well after my big day.

Dad ______________ all day.

Write a **response** to somewhere you have been or something you have seen. Make sure you tell who, what, when and where. Read your text to others in the class. Adjust the **volume**, **pitch** and **pace** of your reading to keep listeners interested. Use eye contact.

Unit 2

Adjectives, clauses

This text is **informative**. The writer tells about their grandparents.

My Grandparents

In 1977, my grandparents came to live in Australia. They were refugees from Vietnam.

When they arrived in Australia, my grandparents had no possessions and they did not speak English. Life was difficult at first, but they were very brave and they worked hard.

My family is proud of our Vietnamese heritage. Our most important celebration is Tết, or New Year. At Tết, we clean the house and we get new clothes and eat special foods. My grandparents, parents and uncle give me 'lucky money'.

I love Tết and I love my grandparents.

Rule An **adjective** can describe.

Tết is my favourite celebration. It is fun.

1 Use **adjectives** from *My Grandparents* to complete the sentences.

Vietnamese New Year is ____________ to the writer's family.

The writer's grandparents were ____________ to come to a new country.

New Year is celebrated with ____________ clothes and ____________ foods.

The writer loves ____________ money.

The grandparents worked ____________.

Life in Australia was ____________ at first.

2 An explorer is a person who sets out to discover new or unfamiliar areas. Would you call the writer's grandparents explorers? Explain.

____

____

3 Underline the **proper nouns** in *My Grandparents*.

Grammar Rules! Student Book 3 (ISBN 9780655092513) © Tanya Gibb

4 List all the **common nouns** used for people in *My Grandparents*.

____

____

5 Write a definition for *refugee*. Use a dictionary.

____

Rule

A **clause** is a unit of meaning that includes a **verb**. A single clause is a **simple sentence**. Sentences begin with a capital letter and end with a full stop, question mark or exclamation mark.

Today is Friday. *Are you busy?* *Stop that!*

6 Underline each group of words that is a **sentence**. Add a full stop, question mark or exclamation mark.

Hard-working grandparents

The dog ate my homework

Bronte and Lee

Will Mum make spring rolls

Dad told me which

7 Unscramble each **sentence**. Rewrite it correctly with **punctuation** marks.

australia mum was born in

____

can vietnam we visit

____

the finish line run to quickly

____

celebrations new year are fun vietnamese

____

Interview a family member. Find out about your family history or a particular celebration your family enjoys. Create a multimodal text to share information about your family with your class.

Unit 3

Personal pronouns, thinking and feeling verbs

This email is a **response** that gives the writer's point of view. It uses **personal pronouns**.

Dear Nana and Pop,

I am excited for the next school holidays. Jack says we will drive up there on the Saturday morning.

I hope Shadow remembers me!

Yesterday, Dad told me that archaeologists have discovered cave art in Australia that was painted 170 000 years ago. I think that is incredible. The discovery means that First Nations Australians lived in Australia much earlier than people knew about.

I miss you.

I LOVE YOU, Hannah

Rule

Personal pronouns are words that refer to or replace **nouns**. They help track a person or thing across a text.

I me we us you he she her him they them it

The dingo ran away because she was frightened.

1 Read *Dear Nana and Pop*. Circle the **personal pronouns**.

2 Write a **personal pronoun** from the box on each line. Circle other personal pronouns in the sentences.

He	me	it	They	She	them	It	you

Will and Kyle are coming on Saturday. __________ are looking forward to it.

Pass the scissors to Gemma. __________ needs __________.

Follow Harry. __________ will show you the way.

A magpie swooped me today. __________ scared __________.

Can I have a mango? I'll share __________ with __________.

Grammar Rules! Student Book 3 (ISBN 9780655092513) © Tanya Gibb

Thinking and **feeling verbs** are verbs for thoughts and feelings.

feel think hope wondered remembered loved

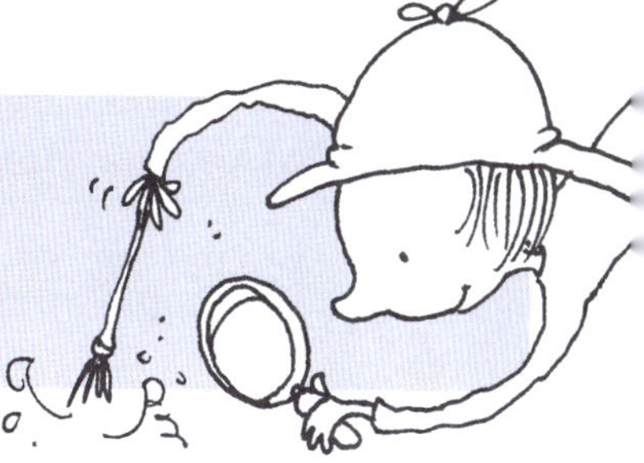

3 Find and underline the **thinking** and **feeling verbs** in *Dear Nana and Pop.*

4 Circle the **thinking** or **feeling verb** in each simple sentence.

I hope Nana and Pop visit us soon.

I forgot my library book today.

I like banana cake best.

I remembered my homework.

Brett decided that he likes broccoli after all.

5 In *Dear Nana and Pop*, where is Jack taking Hannah in the next school holidays?

____

6 Write a **sentence** to answer each question.

How old are you?

____

Who lives with you?

____

What is your favourite food?

____

7 Find a sentence that is an exclamation in *Dear Nana and Pop*. Copy it onto the line.

____

Write a letter or an email to a friend or relative. Tell them about something that you are excited about. Use **thinking** and **feeling verbs** and **personal pronouns**. Take care to punctuate your sentences correctly.

Unit 4

Personal pronouns, noun groups, articles

This text is the beginning of a **mystery narrative**. It uses **noun groups** to describe the setting and main character.

The Case of the Missing Robots

On a peaceful island off the coast of Australia, there lived a clever inventor. The inventor made robots with artificial intelligence. This meant they could think for themselves.

The inventor lived alone. He had no human friends, only the robots, and he loved them.

One day, there was a huge explosion outside the robot factory. The inventor went inside to check on his robots, but he couldn't find a single one. They had completely disappeared.

1 Read *The Case of the Missing Robots.* What might the rest of the story be about?

____

2 Read *The Case of the Missing Robots.* Circle the **personal pronouns**.

What **noun** does *He/he* refer to? ______________

What **noun** do *they* and *them* refer to? ______________

3 Complete each sentence using a **personal pronoun** from the box. Use a capital letter if the **pronoun** begins a sentence.

he	she	they	them

__________ went to find his robots. He couldn't find __________.

__________ were missing. The worried inventor phoned his mother.

__________ told him not to worry.

Grammar Rules! Student Book 3 (ISBN 9780655092513) © Tanya Gibb

4 Complete each sentence. Use the **personal pronouns** from the box. Use a capital letter if the pronoun begins a sentence.

it	it	it	he	them	they

The island is off the coast. __________ is a beautiful place.

The inventor builds robots. __________ invents __________.

A fast boat collects the robots. __________ arrives each month.

The explosion was outside the factory. __________ was very loud.

The robots had vanished. __________ were nowhere to be seen.

Rule

A **noun group** is a group of words that includes a **noun**.
A noun group can begin with an **article** (*a, an, the*). A noun group can include **adjectives** that describe (*the missing robots*) or tell quantity (*two robots, a few years*).

5 Underline four **adjectives** in *The Case of the Missing Robots.*

6 Add a **noun** from *The Case of the Missing Robots* to form **noun groups**.

clever ____________________

peaceful ____________________

huge ____________________

artificial ____________________

7 Draw lines to link each **adjective** to a **noun**.

happy	ghost
angry	pirate
scary	smile
ferocious	voice
whiny	frown

8 Add an **article** and an interesting **adjective** of your own to form **noun groups**.

____________________ spaceship

____________________ discovery

____________________ experiment

____________________ journey

____________________ scientist

____________________ alien

Try it yourself!

Finish the **narrative** *The Case of the Missing Robots*. Why had the robots disappeared? What will the inventor do? How will the story end? Ask a classmate to help you revise your draft before publishing and sharing it with others in the class.

Inventing Potato Chips

This film review is a persuasive text. It is a **response** to a movie. It includes the writer's **opinion**.

I saw a really entertaining movie about the invention of potato chips. A chef in a restaurant in America, in about 1850, made French fries. A customer complained that the fries weren't thin enough. The chef made them thinner and thinner, but the customer said they still weren't thin enough. Finally, the chef fried paper-thin slices and sprinkled them with plenty of salt. The customer said they were fantastic. So that's how potato chips were invented. The movie was very funny. I enjoyed it and I think you would enjoy it too.

Rule

Saying verbs are verbs that show you something has been said.

asked *screamed* *shouted*

1 Read *Inventing Potato Chips*. Underline the **saying verbs**.

2 Write a **saying verb** of your own on the line.

'These chips are fantastic!' ______________ the happy customer.

3 Use a **saying verb** from the box to complete each sentence.

stated	cheered	told	asked	announced

The customer ______________ that the fries were too thick.

The customer ______________ the chef to try again.

The customer ______________ the chef to make the fries thinner.

The customer ______________ the fries were perfect.

The chef ______________ when the customer was happy.

Grammar Rules! Student Book 3 (ISBN 9780655092513) © Tanya Gibb

4 Write a sentence for each **saying verb** in the box.

whispered yelled cried	

Tip Film and book reviews use **thinking** and **feeling verbs** to express opinions.

5 Write the sentence from *Inventing Potato Chips* that uses a **thinking** or **feeling verb** to tell you the writer's opinion.

____

6 Finish the sentence.

The writer said the movie was ______________________________.

7 Write *fact* or *opinion* after each sentence.

I loved the movie. ____________

Potato chips are healthy. ____________

Potato chips are made from potatoes. ____________

Chefs must be clever at inventing new recipes. ____________

Everyone loves potato chips. ____________

8 Write a **fact** about your class.

____

9 Write an **opinion** about your class.

____

Write a review of a movie, book or television show that you have enjoyed or a song you like. Write your opinions about it. Use **thinking** and **feeling verbs** and **adjectives**.

Unit 6 Revision

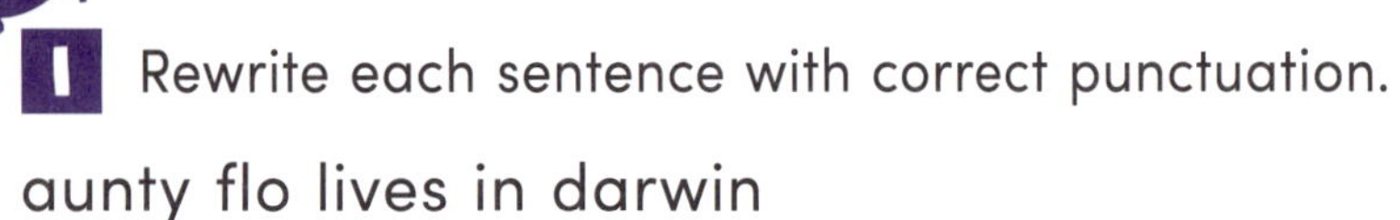

1 Rewrite each sentence with correct punctuation.

aunty flo lives in darwin

____

today is wednesday

____

school holidays begin in april

____

2 Write eight **common nouns** for things in your classroom.

____

____

3 Underline the **doing verbs** in the box.

jumped	house	science	island	invented	cooked

4 Write a **sentence** telling what each animal did.

____

____

____

5 Unscramble each **thinking** or **feeling verb**.

ovedl ______________ tedha ______________ beedliev ______________

pohed ______________ shiwde ______________ eedend ______________

Grammar Rules! Student Book 3 (ISBN 9780655092513) © Tanya Gibb

6 Complete each sentence with a **personal pronoun** from the box. Use a capital letter if the pronoun begins a sentence.

we	us	they	them

Give ________ their books.

________ can come with us.

________ enjoy watching movies together.

Will you watch the movie with ________?

7 Unjumble the words and write the **sentences**. Use correct punctuation.

potato tasty I think chips are

____

pancakes I love for breakfast to eat

____

going you the are to watch movie

____

away go

____

8 Form **noun groups**. Draw a line to link an **adjective** to each **noun**.

cute	island
sore	king
bossy	dog
old	knee
beautiful	kitten

9 Write *fact* or *opinion* after each sentence.

Computers are machines. ____________

All sharks are scary. ____________

I love broccoli. ____________

Magpies are birds. ____________

10 Complete each sentence with a **saying verb**.

The mother ______________ to her baby.

The scientist ______________ everyone about her discovery.

The chef ______________ with the customer.

Team members ______________ when they won.

Unit 7

Prepositional phrases, adjectives

My special place
at the bottom of the yard,
under scraggy bushes,
through prickly hedges,
into a dark tunnel,
beneath the overgrowth –
still and quiet.
Secret place –
discovered and hidden.

The poet uses **prepositional phrases** with **adjectives** to describe the setting.

Rule

A **prepositional phrase** is a preposition (e.g. *in, on, under, over, by, at*) linked to a **noun, noun group** or **pronoun**. A phrase can tell where or when an activity takes place or with whom or what. A phrase does not include a verb.

beside the creek   *at 5 o'clock*   *over it*   *with jam*

1 Read *My Special Place*. Circle the **prepostional phrases** that tell where.

2 Use a word from the box to make **phrases** in each **sentence**.

over	under	behind	through	on

Jump ______________ the fence.

Look ______________ the rug.

Crawl ______________ the tunnel.

Sit ______________ the log.

Hide it ______________ your back.

3 Circle all the words that could be used in this sentence.

I crawled ____________ the branch.

over	through	into	beside	from	around	above	along

Grammar Rules! Student Book 3 (ISBN 9780655092513) © Tanya Gibb

4 Circle all the words that could be used in this sentence.

I looked __________ the fence.

during	near	towards	under	around	without	before	beyond

5 Write **phrases** that tell where or when to complete the sentences.

Let's go to the park ______________________________.

We'll eat the popcorn ______________________________.

Brush your teeth ______________________________.

The movie starts ______________________________.

6 Complete each sentence with a **prepositional phrase** to tell where.

The lorikeets chattered ______________________________.

The dog squeezed ______________________________.

The tiger prowled ______________________________.

The worms wriggled ______________________________.

7 Underline the **adjectives** in *My Special Place.*

8 Write new **adjectives** to give a different description of the special place.

Tip Remember the rule on page 10.

under ______________ bushes

through ______________ hedges

into a ______________ tunnel

9 Write two **adjectives** to describe each **noun**.

______________ ______________ apple

______________ ______________ bedroom

______________ ______________ mango

______________ ______________ hamburger

Try it yourself!

Write a **poem** about a special place where you like to go. It could be a cubbyhouse, your local park or somewhere in your home. Use **prepositional phrases** to tell where. Use interesting **adjectives** to describe your special place.

Unit 8

Main idea, contractions, possessive apostrophes

This **persuasive** text presents the author's opinion and reasons.

Use Less Plastic!

Plastic is a very useful invention, but it has become a huge problem in the environment.

Plastic doesn't rot and decompose to feed the earth like plant and animal matter. Large pieces of plastic choke animals or the animals get entangled in it and die. In the environment, plastic breaks down into smaller and smaller pieces that we can't see. These tiny pieces are in the air, in dirt and dust, in our water and our oceans, in our food and even in us.

Plastic can be recycled but most of it isn't. It just ends up as pollution and plastic lasts forever. People should use less plastic!

Rule The **main idea** in a text is the idea the author wants you to accept or believe.

1 What is the **main idea** in *Use Less Plastic!*? To identify the main idea ask: What is it that the author wants me to accept?

____

2 What reasons does the author of *Use Less Plastic!* give to support the **main idea**?

____

____

3 Write six **prepositional phrases** that tell <u>where</u> in *Use Less Plastic!*.

____

____

4 Find two **adjectives** in *Use Less Plastic!* that are opposite in meaning.

____

Grammar Rules! Student Book 3 (ISBN 9780655092513) © Tanya Gibb

5 Find **adjectives** in *Use Less Plastic!* to complete the **noun groups**.

Plastic is a very ____________ invention but also a ____________ problem.

Rule

Apostrophes are used in **contractions** to show that letters have been left out.

do not → *don't* *it is* → *it's* *I am* *I'm*

6 Write three **contractions** used in *Use Less Plastic!*. Then write them in their full forms.

____________ ____________ ____________

____________ ____________ ____________

7 Choose the correct **contraction** from the box. Write it on the line.

She's It's I'll You'll

________ (You will) love the concert.

________ (It is) a Yellow Monday cicada.

________ (I will) help you.

________ (She is) coming by train.

8 Draw a line to link each **contraction** to the full words.

can't	will not
shouldn't	cannot
aren't	should not
won't	did not
didn't	are not

Rule

Apostrophes are used to show possession.

For singular nouns use *'s*: *Jed's book, Ella's hat.*

For plural nouns use *s'*: *the teachers own the cars* → *the teachers' cars.*

If the noun ends in *s* you don't need to add another *s*. *Tess' dog* or *Tess's dog.*

9 Write the noun on each line to show **possession**. Use an **apostrophe**.

Shalesh lives there. That's ____________ house.

Many dogs were barking. The ____________ barking annoyed us.

Ross owns that ball. That's ____________ ball.

Try it yourself!

Create a **persuasive** text. What is the **main idea** you want your readers/listeners to accept? What reasons or evidence will you use to support your main idea? Present your text to your class.

Unit 9

Statements, questions, relating verbs, adverbs

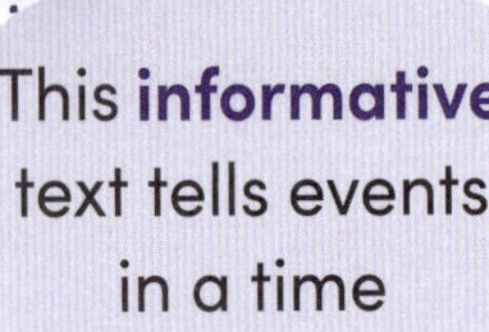

Penicillin

In 1928, a Scottish scientist named Alexander Fleming was studying bacteria growth. Bacteria are germs that can cause infections in people. Fleming discovered that a mould had grown on one of his dishes and that bacteria could not grow where there was mould. He wrote a report about his discovery.

Later, Dr Howard Florey, an Australian, developed penicillin as a medical treatment to kill bacteria. Since then, penicillin has saved millions of lives.

In 1945, Howard Florey, Ernst Chain and Alexander Fleming received the Nobel Peace Prize for Medicine for their work with penicillin.

Rule

A **statement** gives information or an opinion. It ends in a full stop.

Marie Curie was a scientist. *I think Marie Curie was brilliant.*

A **question** asks for information or an opinion. It ends in a question mark.

What is penicillin? *Do you think germs are dangerous?*

1 Read *Penicillin*. Write a **statement** to answer each **question**.

When was Alexander Fleming studying bacteria growth?

____

What are bacteria?

____

Who discovered penicillin?

____

Where was Howard Florey from?

____

How does penicillin work?

____

Grammar Rules! Student Book 3 (ISBN 9780655092513) © Tanya Gibb

2 Write a **question** for each answer.

I hid the treasure in a cave.

I go to bed at 8 pm.

______________________ ______________________

______________________ ______________________

Rule **Relating (being) verbs** show relationships, such as being and having. You cannot see any action taking place. *is are have has had was*

3 Add a **relating verb** from the box to each sentence.

was is are has had

Bacteria ________ germs.

Marie Curie ________ a scientist a long time ago.

What ________ penicillin?

Dillon ________ an allergy to penicillin.

Annie ________ penicillin last month for an infection.

Rule **Adverbs** can **sequence** events in time and tell <u>when</u>.

then now yesterday soon later always often rarely

4 Find three phrases in *Penicillin* that show **time** or sequence.

______________ ______________ ______________

5 Use a **time word** from the box to complete each sentence.

soon now later tomorrow

The alarm clock will go off ______________.

Shall we go ______________?

I'll show you ______________.

The expedition leaves ______________.

Choose an event from the past that interests you. Write **questions** that you have about the event. Research the event and write a report. Sequence information in time order.

Unit 10

Conjunctions, singular and plural nouns, suffixes

Molly's Discovery

The sand squished between Oliver's toes. He was playing fetch with his dog, Molly, at the beach. It was a hot day. The beach was crowded, so Oliver and Molly went farther along the beach than usual. They went farther than they had ever ventured before, to the northern end, where nobody ever went. Oliver threw the ball, but when Molly returned, the ball was not in her mouth. In her mouth was a small casket. Molly dropped it at Oliver's feet. Oliver bent down for a closer look. He picked it up and he dusted off the sand. He lifted the lid.

This text is the **orientation** for a **narrative.** It uses **noun groups** for the characters and the setting.

Rule **Conjunctions** are words that link words, phrases and clauses in sentences (*and, so, because, or, but*). Two **independent clauses** linked by a conjunction form a **compound sentence.** *I like carrot cake but I prefer banana cake.*

1 Read *Molly's Discovery.* Circle the compound sentence that uses the **conjunction** *and.*

2 Use a **conjunction** to join each pair of simple sentences. Write the new sentences on the lines.

Oliver took Molly to the beach. She likes to swim.

____

Oliver threw the ball. Molly did not fetch it.

____

Molly took off down the beach. Oliver ran after her.

____

Molly dropped the casket in the sand. Oliver dusted it off.

____

3 Use the **conjunctions** from the box to join the **clauses** in the sentences.

because but or

Give it back __________ I will be upset with you.

Give it back __________ I want a turn.

You can have a turn __________ I want another turn.

Grammar Rules! Student Book 3 (ISBN 9780655092513) © Tanya Gibb

A **noun** can be **singular** or **plural**.

dog→dogs *beach→beaches* *mouse→mice* *person→people*

Note that words ending in *y* change *y* to *i* to add *-es* *berry→berries*

Some nouns don't change at all from singular to plural. *fish* *sheep*

4 Write the **plural** of each **singular noun**.

crowd ______________ adventure ______________ beach ______________

box ______________ battery ______________ city ______________

toe ______________ casket ______________ mouth ______________

5 Write the **singular** of each **plural noun**.

people ______________ feet ______________ men ______________

women ______________ leaves ______________ lollies ______________

6 What can you tell about the relationship between Molly and Oliver in *Molly's Discovery?* Explain.

____

____

In a clause, the **verb** needs to agree with the **subject**.

The dog plays. *The dogs play.*

The dog was running. *The dogs were running.*

7 Cross out the incorrect **verb** in each sentence.

Abby (run/runs) faster than her brother.

The boys (swims/swim) very quickly.

The children (eat/eats) lunch at midday.

What will Oliver find in the casket? Finish the **narrative**. Vary the lengths of your sentences to build descriptions or to add suspense. You could create a storyboard for a film of the narrative.

Unit 11

Exclamations, adverbs, onomatopoeia

This text is an **orientation** for a **narrative**. It introduces the main character and the setting. **Adverbs, adjectives** and **onomatopoeia** help to make the story interesting.

Search for the Lost Valley

Crack! Snap! Alex carelessly stomped over the fallen branches as she trudged through the forest. She was searching to discover a lost valley. Legend said it was somewhere nearby. She plodded on angrily because she had searched for days, unsuccessfully. She was beginning to think she was on a wild goose chase. It was so hot, sticky and humid that she decided to have a rest. She found a fallen log and sat down heavily. In the silence that followed, she could suddenly hear the unmistakable sound of running water over a waterfall. It was her hidden valley!

Rule

An **exclamation** is a word or sentence that shows strong emotion, or gives a warning or command. It ends in an exclamation mark.

Stop! *Look at that!* *I love it!*

1 Read *Search for the Lost Valley*. Underline three **exclamations**.

2 Write an **exclamation** for Alex to shout as she:

stomped on a fallen branch ____________________

plodded angrily ____________________

heard the waterfall ____________________

3 Write an **exclamation** for each picture.

____________________ ____________________

____________________ ____________________

Grammar Rules! Student Book 3 (ISBN 9780655092513) © Tanya Gibb

Some **adverbs** add meaning to **verbs** by telling how.

quickly *suddenly* *happily* *busily* *carefully*

Adverbs can also tell where. *here* *there* *up* *down*

4 Write five **adverbs** ending in *–ly* from *Search for the Lost Valley.*

____

5 Use an **adverb** from the box to complete each sentence.

fiercely wildly down carefully

The children sat ______________.

The wind blew ______________.

The child carried the puppy ______________.

The lion growled ______________.

6 Find and circle the verbs *stomped, trudged* and *plodded* in *Search for the Lost Valley*. What do these **doing verbs** tell you about Alex's attitude?

____

7 Write two **prepositional phrases** that tell you where Alex walked in *Search for the Lost Valley.*

____

Rule

Onomatopoeia is the name for words that imitate sounds.

Onomatopoeia words can help to add atmosphere to a narrative.

bang *crash* *pop* *fizz* *slurp* *kerplunk*

8 Find two **onomatopoeia** words in *Search for the Lost Valley.* ______________ ______________

9 Write an **onomatopoeia** word for a sound made by each thing.

a dog ______________ a cat ______________

a snake ______________ sausages frying in a pan ______________

Try it yourself!

Write a **narrative** of your own. Include **onomatopoeia** words to represent sounds. Add **exclamations** to show when characters are angry, excited or surprised. Use **adverbs** to tell how actions happen.

Unit 12 Revision

1 Write the **contractions**.

cannot __________ he is __________

would not __________ I am __________

you will __________ do not __________

they are __________ it will __________

2 Circle the correct **verb** for the **subject** of each sentence.

A kookaburra (laugh/laughs).

Kookaburras (laugh/laughs).

Amira (eat/eats) faster than me.

They (read/reads) more often than me.

3 Write a **prepositional phrase** to complete each sentence.

I like to swim ______________________________.

I wear a hat ______________________________.

The mice jumped ______________________________.

I keep my tools ______________________________.

4 Write two **adjectives** to describe each **noun**.

__________________ __________________ chimpanzee

__________________ __________________ banana

__________________ __________________ gadget

5 Choose a **relating verb** from the box to complete each sentence.

is	was	have	are

Elephants __________ trunks.

Whales __________ mammals.

Igor __________ my friend.

I __________ on the phone.

6 Cross out the incorrect **personal pronoun** in each sentence.

They will take me with (they/them) to the park.

(She/Her) is a great goalkeeper.

(It/He) is a good cook.

The book is Billy's. Give (it/them) back.

Nonna went skydiving with (him/he).

7 Write an **exclamation** that shows:

surprise ____

a warning ____

Grammar Rules! Student Book 3 (ISBN 9780655092513) © Tanya Gibb

8 Add a **possessive apostrophe** to the noun in brackets to complete each sentence.

(Irina) *Irina's* batting is the best.

That's (Ross) ____________ ball.

That's my (teacher) ____________ new desk.

The (team) ____________ win was amazing.

(Xiao) ____________ homework is on his bed.

The (dogs) ____________ barking annoyed us.

9 Use a **conjunction** from the box to complete each sentence.

so and or because

I won't be able to sleep ____________ I am excited.

It's Dom's birthday ____________ I will make him a cake.

I made chocolate cake ____________ Ariana made Anzac biscuits.

You can have custard ____________ you can have ice cream.

10 Use a **conjunction** from the box to join each pair of sentences. Write the new sentences.

because	except

I love playing netball. I am a good goal shooter.

____

It can come inside. The dog cannot come inside when it has muddy feet.

____

11 Write the **plural** of each **singular noun** so that there is more than one.

person ____________ shoe ____________ monkey ____________

12 Write the **singular** of each **plural noun** so that there is only one of each thing.

teeth ____________ cookies ____________ wishes ____________

13 Use an **adverb** from the box to complete each sentence.

happily slowly quickly lazily

The old cat yawned ____________.

The children played ____________.

The birthday cake was eaten ____________.

The tortoise plodded ____________ across the sand.

Unit 13

Quoted speech, saying verbs

Trampolines

'Dad,' asked Henry, 'do you think the trampoline was a good invention?'

'I'd say that jumping on a trampoline is great exercise, as much fun as jumping on the bed but definitely safer than jumping on the bed,' Dad suggested. 'What do you think?'

'I really like jumping on the bed but I'm not allowed,' reminded Henry.

'You certainly are NOT allowed to jump on the bed. Jumping on the bed is dangerous with all the furniture nearby, so it's just as well the trampoline was invented,' lectured Dad.

This text is a **discussion**. Each person makes statements that tell their point of view.

Rule

Quoted speech is the actual speech someone says. It is written inside **quotation (speech) marks**.

'What do you think?' asked Dad.

1 Read *Trampolines*. Highlight the words that Dad says. Use a different colour to highlight the words that Henry says.

2 Work with a partner. One of you say Dad's speech. One of you say Henry's speech. Then add some extra **questions** and **statements** to their **discussion**.

3 Write what Henry would say next as **quoted speech**.

____

4 Write what Dad would say next as **quoted speech**.

____

5 Add **quotation marks** to show which words are said. The quotation marks enclose any other punctuation marks. You can use single or double quotation marks.

I want a turn! shouted Billy.

That's so funny, giggled Marie.

Dad whispered, Santa Claus might bring a trampoline.

Can I have a turn? begged Yan.

Grammar Rules! Student Book 3 (ISBN 9780655092513) © Tanya Gibb

6 Write the **saying verbs** used in *Trampolines* for

Dad's speech ________________ ________________

Henry's speech ________________ ________________

7 Circle the **saying verbs** in the box.

whispered	yelled	swam	whined	laughed	asked	peeped

Use one of the **saying verbs** in the box in a sentence of your own.

____

Tip

Adjectives, **verbs** and **adverbs** show a speaker's or writer's **evaluation** of a topic and can influence the way a listener or reader thinks about a topic.

<u>hilarious</u> film *<u>brave</u> explorer* *Rasha <u>sighed wearily</u>.*

8 What is Dad's opinion about trampolines?

____

What is Dad's opinion about jumping on the bed?

____

9 Find three **contractions** in *Trampolines*.

________________ ________________ ________________

10 Write **contractions** for the words.

is not ________________ can not ________________

would have ________________ should have ________________

I will ________________ you will ________________

Try it yourself!

Discuss your favourite game or activity with a partner. Record part of the **discussion**. Use **quotation marks** to show what was said. Use a variety of **saying verbs**.

Unit 14

Point of view, emotive words, modal verbs and adverbs

This text is from a **narrative**. It includes a conversation where one character is trying to **persuade** the other to do something. Each person's speech is a new paragraph.

THE THING INSIDE

'No Deni, I really don't want to go in there,' argued Amy.

'Don't be a chicken. We might discover treasure, and it will be fun,' Deni fumed.

'You've heard the stories about that house! What if they're true? Also, it's trespassing,' Amy explained, with her arms folded in front of her.

'What if? What if? What if? Look, the fact is, there is absolutely no such thing as a ghost,' Deni announced convincingly. 'So, stay here or come with me but I'm going in.'

Deni walked up the front steps of the derelict old house. The floorboards creaked and groaned at her every step. She stopped at the front door and turned back towards Amy.

'Well?' she asked, raising her eyebrows.

Tip **Body language** and **voice** are often used in arguments to reinforce the point of view. Body language includes gestures and facial expressions. Voice includes volume, pace and tone (the sound of your voice).

1 Read *The Thing Inside*. Highlight the words that Deni says. Use a different colour to highlight what Amy says.

2 Work with a partner. One of you say Deni's speech. One of you say Amy's speech. Use **body language** and **voice** to reinforce their points of view.

3 What **body language** does Amy use in *The Thing Inside*?

____

What do you think her **body language** means?

____

4 What **body language** does Deni use in *The Thing Inside*?

____

What do you think her **body language** means?

____

5 Write Amy's point of view and reasons. Write Deni's point of view and reasons.

Amy	**Deni**
______________________	______________________
______________________	______________________

Would you prefer Amy or Deni as a friend? Why?

____

Rule

Modal verbs (e.g. *should, might, must, will, can*) and **adverbs** (e.g. *possibly, probably, always, rarely*) are used to make statements more or less forceful, certain or convincing.

You might. *You must not.*

You probably should. *You definitely shouldn't.*

6 Tick the sentence in each pair that makes a stronger argument.

I really love pizzas. ☐	I love pizzas. ☐
I want to go. ☐	I think I want to go. ☐
It's probably haunted. ☐	It's definitely haunted. ☐
It might not be yours. ☐	It is not yours. ☐

7 What might the *thing* inside be? What could happen next in the narrative?

____

____

Work with a partner. Choose a topic to **argue** about. Take opposite points of view. Express your points of view very strongly but respectfully. Use **modal verbs** and **adverbs**, **voice** and **body language** to look and sound convincing.

Unit

15

Commas, possessive pronouns, word families

This text is part of a biography. A biography tells about a person's life.

Jane Goodall

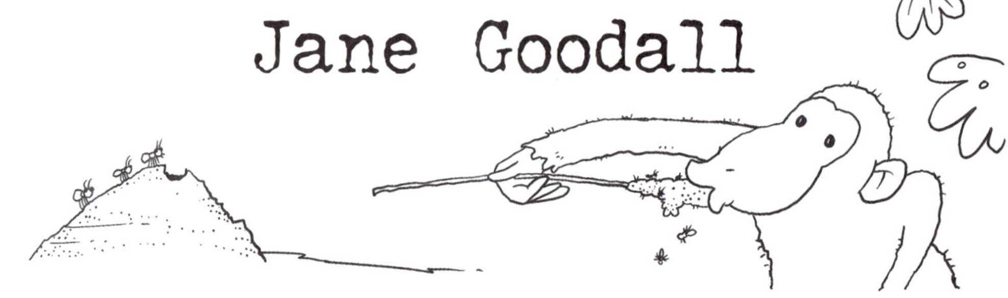

Jane Goodall is famous for her discoveries about wild chimpanzees in Tanzania, Africa.

Jane began studying chimpanzee behaviour in 1960. She was the first person to notice wild chimpanzees make and use tools. She saw the chimps strip leaves off sticks and poke the sticks into termite mounds, digging out the termites to eat. Until Jane's discovery, it was thought that only humans made or used tools. Jane also discovered that chimpanzees feel emotions and have personalities. No scientists had ever noted that before.

Jane later founded charities for wildlife research and to save wild chimpanzees and their habitat.

1 Read *Jane Goodall.* What did Jane discover about chimpanzees?

____

____

2 Why do you think Jane Goodall set up a charity to save the chimpanzees' habitat?

____

Possessive pronouns are pronouns that show possession.

mine ours yours theirs his hers its

That hat is mine. The forest is theirs. These seats are ours.

3 Write a **possessive pronoun** on each line.

Jane's discovery was important. The credit for the discovery is ________________.

Those chimpanzees think that termite mound is ________________.

Grammar Rules! Student Book 3 (ISBN 9780655092513) © Tanya Gibb

Commas separate items in a series. *Bring pens, pencils, paper and a ruler.*
Commas separate quoted speech. *'Hello,' said Madison.* OR *Madison said, 'Hello.'*

4 Rewrite each sentence with correct **punctuation**.

how did jane become interested in chimpanzees

____

chimpazees eat fruit seeds nuts flowers and insects

____

id like to help save bilbies from extinction said lachie

____

elijah swiftly overtook jackson mo and jade in the race

____

5 In *Jane Goodall*, find the sentence *No scientists had ever noted that before.* What does the word *that* refer to?

____

6 Write an **adverb** from the box on each line.

clearly swiftly famously cleverly

The chimp ________________ poked the stick in the mound.
The termites ________________ ran out of the mound.
Jane ________________ understood the need for wild animal protection.
Jane ________________ discovered that chimps make and use tools.

Words in a family have the same base. *hope, hopes, hopeful, hopefully, hopeless*

7 Write a **word family** for *discover*.

____

____

A **biography** is an account of someone's life written by someone else.
An **autobiography** is when someone creates an account of their own life.
Create your autobiography.

This **advertisement** uses **emotive words** to persuade people to buy a product.

Wiz Bang 3000 Kitchen Hand!

Have you ever needed a spare hand in the kitchen?
Do you often run out of time to chop your food?
Do you ever run out of time to cook your food?
Do you ever run out of time to clean up the mess and do the dishes?
Do you ever wonder if you will have enough time to eat your food?
We now have the answer for you:

The WIZ BANG 3000 KITCHEN HAND!

It chops, cooks, cleans and also feeds you your food.
Just ask for a meal from your WIZ BANG 3000 KITCHEN HAND and it will do everything.
Be quick! The WIZ BANG 3000 KITCHEN HAND has almost sold out.
Hurry! Get this **amazing** invention today!

Don't miss out! Buy now!

Tip **Emotive words** are used in advertisements to persuade people to buy something.

1. Read *Wiz Bang 3000 Kitchen Hand!*. Underline the **emotive words** that might convince a reader to buy one straight away.

2. *Wiz Bang 3000 Kitchen Hand!* uses the **emotive words** *'Don't miss out'*. How do you feel when you miss out on something that you really want?

____

____

Grammar Rules! Student Book 3 (ISBN 9780655092513) © Tanya Gibb

A **command** is a sentence that tells someone to do something.
A command often begins with a verb. *Wash your hands.*

3 Write five **commands** used in *Wiz Bang 3000 Kitchen Hand!*.

____

____

____

4 What does the advertisement claim that the Wiz Bang 3000 Kitchen Hand can do?

____

____

5 Tick the statements that show certainty.

- [ ] I will have a lunch order today.
- [ ] You might like to come.
- [ ] You must hug your teddy.
- [ ] I might have toast for breakfast.
- [ ] They will be late.

6 The first part of the advertisement asks the reader a series of questions. Talk with a partner. What is the purpose of the questions?

____

____

7 In *Wiz Bang 3000 Kitchen Hand!* circle the **personal pronouns** that address the reader.

8 Find the **personal pronouns** that refer to the Wiz Bang 3000 Kitchen Hand. Underline them in red.

9 Find the **personal pronoun** that refers to the makers of the Wiz Bang 3000 Kitchen Hand. Underline it in blue.

Remember the rule on page 12.

Write an **advertisement** for a household appliance. Use a real appliance, such as a toaster or an electric toothbrush, or invent a new appliance. Use **modal verbs** and **adverbs** and **emotive words** to convince people to buy your appliance.

The purpose of this text is to describe bush tucker and persuade the reader to try it.

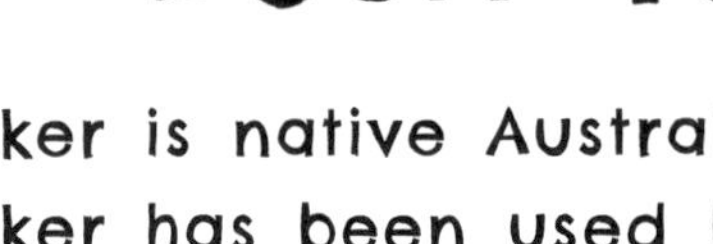

BUSH TUCKER

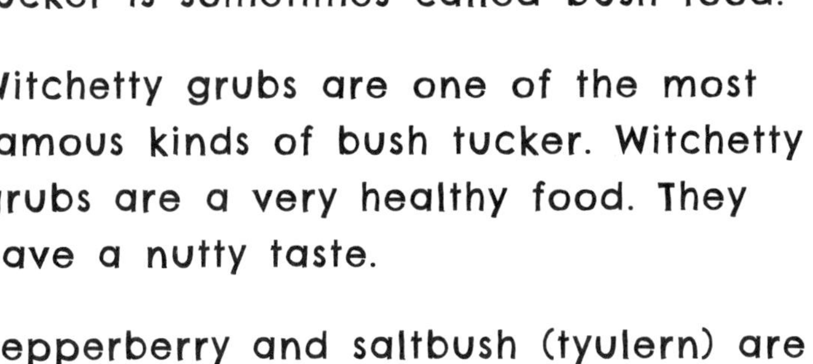

Bush tucker is native Australian food. Bush tucker has been used by First Nations Australians for tens of thousands of years for food and medicines. Bush tucker is sometimes called bush food.

Witchetty grubs are one of the most famous kinds of bush tucker. Witchetty grubs are a very healthy food. They have a nutty taste.

Pepperberry and saltbush (tyulern) are bush foods. They taste just like salt and pepper but are healthier.

A very popular kind of bush tucker is the Davidson's plum or ooray. Ooray are a darker purple than other plums and they make the best jam.

Tip Remember the rule about **noun groups** with **articles** on page 15.

1 Read *Bush Tucker*. Underline four **noun groups** that begin with an **article**.

2 Circle the correct **article** in each **sentence**.

I tried (a / an) Davidson's plum.

It had (a / an) amazingly intense flavour.

It had (a / an) dark purple colour.

(The / An / A) plum was cut in half.

(The / A / An) Davidson's plum jam was delicious.

3 Which bush tucker does the writer of *Bush Tucker* think tastes like nuts?

Grammar Rules! Student Book 3 (ISBN 9780655092513) © Tanya Gibb

Grammar Rules!

_______________ 's Writing Log

1 Plan

What is the purpose of the writing?
Who is the audience?
What type of text and text form will you use? How can you enhance the presentation?
Gather ideas or research the topic, including using online and digital sources.

2 Draft

Gather and organise your ideas.
Use a graphic organiser or digital tools.
Compose your text.

3 Edit/Revise

Check your work for meaning, clarity and precision.
Is the structure and sequencing appropriate?
Check layout, paragraphing and sentence structures.
Check topic specific vocabulary.
Ask for help to improve meaning and precision.

4 Proofread

Check grammar and punctuation.
Check homophones are correct.
Use online dictionaries to check spelling.

5 Publish

Use layout and visual features.
Use digital tools.
Reflect on your work and your text.

Create symbols for a rating scale. Then each time you finish a piece of writing, record it in the log.

My rating scale

Symbol	Meaning
	Help!
	A good start.
	I have the basics covered.
	I'm beyond the basics.
	Brilliant!

Do you need some ideas for other text forms to try? Look at the back page!

Date	Write the title of your text.	Text purpose and structure	Audience
Write the date.	Write the title of your piece.	e.g. recount/ email	Who were you writing <u>for</u> or <u>to</u>?

Grammar Rules! Student Book 3 (ISBN 9780655092513) © Tanya Gibb

Language features	My rating	Where to next?
ist the main grammar and other language eatures that you used.	Record your rating.	What grammar could you try next? How could you improve your writing? Does your teacher have any comments?

I've tried these types of texts and text forms . . .

Narrative

- [ ] Poem
- [ ] Retelling a story
- [ ] Other ______________

Recount

- [ ] Letter/email
- [ ] News article
- [ ] A real or imagined event
- [ ] Other ______________

Description

- [ ] Poem
- [ ] Wanted poster/lost poster
- [ ] Letter
- [ ] Advertisement
- [ ] Narrative/story

Response

- [ ] Diary
- [ ] Review (book, concert, excursion)
- [ ] Poem
- [ ] Other ______________

Persuasion

- [ ] Debate
- [ ] Argument/speech
- [ ] Advertisement
- [ ] Poster
- [ ] Poem
- [ ] Other ______________

Informative

- [ ] Information report
- [ ] Brochure/poster
- [ ] Autobiography
- [ ] Other ______________

Explanation

- [ ] Cycle diagram/flow chart
- [ ] Poster

Procedure

- [ ] Recipe
- [ ] Instructions
- [ ] Rules
- [ ] Directions

Discussion

- [ ] Conversation
- [ ] Narrative dialogue
- [ ] Formal interview
- [ ] Other ______________

Grammar Rules! Student Book 3 (ISBN 9780655092513) © Tanya Gibb

Adjectives change form when used to compare things.
When comparing two things we often add *–er*.

long→longer

When comparing more than two things we often add *–est*.

long→longer→longest

4 Write the different forms for each **adjective** to compare things.

long	longer	longest
tall		
sweet		
small		
good		

Some **longer adjectives** need a different way to show **comparison**.
Adjectives with more than two syllables usually use:

- *more* for two things *The rose is more beautiful than the dandelion.*
- *most* for more than two things *The rose is the most beautiful flower in the garden.*

5 Complete each **sentence** with *more* or *most.*

Wattle seeds are ____________ delicious than linseeds.

Wattle seeds are the ____________ delicious seeds to use in cakes.

Witchetty grubs are the ____________ famous bush tucker.

Witchetty grubs are ____________ famous than pepperberries.

6 Write the **comparing** forms of these **adjectives**. Hint! You'll find them in *Bush Tucker.*

dark ____________________ healthy ____________________

Write a **description** of an animal or food. Use **noun groups** with **articles** and **adjectives** to build up your description. Be careful to use the right form when using adjectives to compare.

Unit 18 Revision

1 Add **quotation (speech) marks** around the **quoted speech**.

Take me with you! screamed Louie.

I would like to go, too, suggested Rhami.

I think that's a good idea, replied Pop.

Marty sniggered, Good.

2 What does Dad say? Use **quotation marks**.

____

____

What does Mum say? Use **quotation marks**.

____

____

3 Write a **contraction** for each word or word group. Hint! Remember to use an **apostrophe**.

I am ____________

cannot ____________

I have ____________

could have ____________

do not ____________

is not ____________

4 Which sentences express the greatest **certainty**? Tick one box in each row.

I am very pleased. ☐

I am pleased. ☐

I might go. ☐

I will go. ☐

I think I lost my ball. ☐

I lost my ball. ☐

Dad might be home soon. ☐

Dad will be home soon. ☐

5 Tick the **commands**.

Order your lunch by 9 am. ☐

Don't walk on the grass. ☐

Have you thrown out your rubbish? ☐

Put on your sunhat. ☐

6 Circle the **modal verb** in each sentence.

You must sit.

We might go for a walk.

You could try this plum.

We should go for a walk.

Grammar Rules! Student Book 3 (ISBN 9780655092513) © Tanya Gibb

7 Add a **possessive apostrophe** to the noun in brackets for each sentence to show possession.

(Lee) ______________ painting

(Nina) ______________ desk

(Dad) ______________ sock

the (team) ______________ win

(Hilda) ______________ brother

(parents) ______________ applause

8

Try Jitto. You might like it.

Buy Jetto. It tastes great and is good for you.

Which poster above is more **persuasive**? Give reasons for your choice.

____

____

9 Complete the table with **adjectives** that compare.

tall	taller	tallest
loud		
smart		
kind		

10 Write the correct form of the **adjective** in brackets.

One clown was ______________ (funny) than the other.

The clown in the red hat was the ______________ (funny).

My laboratory was ______________ (tidy) than my assistant's.

My laboratory is the ______________ (tidy) laboratory in the building.

11 Write a strong **argument** for Anton to respond to Lena.
'Anton, you have to do my homework. I don't have time,' said Lena.

____

____

Unit 19

Imagery, idiom, simile

Haiku

Haiku poems were invented in Japan.
A haiku poem has 17 syllables in three lines.

Line 1 has 5 syllables.
Line 2 has 7 syllables.
Line 3 has 5 syllables.

Traditional haiku poems are usually about nature. Modern haiku poems can be about any topic and poets can vary the number of syllables they use.

1 Snow floats softly down
whispering on my cold skin.
Winter is here now.

2 See the spring garden.
Listen to magpies warbling.
Flowers fill the air.

3 Raining cats and dogs.
Puddles grow on swampy lawn.
I watch from inside.

4 As fast as lightning,
the eagle swoops on its prey.
Today it will eat.

This text is **informative**. It describes the form of a haiku poem and includes examples of the poem.

Rule

Imagery means using words that appeal to the senses and help a reader or listener create a picture in their mind.

1 What picture do you see in your mind when reading poem 1?

____

2 Write three words from poem 1 that tell you about the weather.

__________ __________ __________

3 What human behaviour does the poet say snow can do in poem 1? __________

4 Which two words tell you snow is quiet in poem 1? __________ __________

5 Which senses does poem 2 appeal to?

__________ __________ __________

Grammar Rules! Student Book 3 (ISBN 9780655092513) © Tanya Gibb

An **idiom** is an expression that means something different from the meaning of the words.

ankle biter *spit the dummy* *put a sock in it*

6 Write the **idiom** used in poem 3. What does it mean?

____

7 Draw a line to link each **idiom** with its meaning.

fit as a fiddle	something worthwhile
shake a leg	die
nothing to sneeze at	very healthy
a dog's breakfast	stranded
kick the bucket	hurry up
high and dry	a mess

8 What do you think the *swampy lawn* in poem 3 feels like and sounds like? Use **adjectives** of your own.

____

____

____

____

____

9 What does the poet reveal in the last line of poem 3?

____

Tip

A **simile** is a figure of speech. Something is spoken of as being <u>like</u> something else. The words *like* or *as* are used.

as quick as a fox *like a tiger*

10 Write the simile in poem 4. ______________________________

11 Draw a line to complete each **simile**.

slept like	a feather
as light as	a log
the ship tossed like	a bee
as busy as	a cork

12 Find five **adverbs** or **prepositional phrases** that tell <u>where</u> or <u>when</u> in the haiku poems.

____

____

____

Try it yourself!

Interview teachers and family members. Ask them to suggest **idioms** and **similes**. Write a poem that uses one or more of their suggestions. Or, create a poster or multimodal text that illustrates one or more.

This is a **speech**. The speaker's purpose is to **persuade** people to do something.

RECYCLE!

Good morning. I'm here today to tell you how important it is to recycle mobile phones.

Firstly, recycling a mobile phone means that all the materials that have gone into making the phone can be recovered and used again instead of wasted. This protects nature because we won't have to mine for new resources.

Secondly, recycling helps save wildlife. For example, coltan is a mineral used in smartphones. Mining for coltan in the Congo Basin in Africa is destroying gorilla habitat. Some gorilla species are in danger of extinction because of loss of habitat.

Additionally, when mobile phones end up in landfill, their batteries leak harmful toxins into the environment.

Help the planet! Recycle your old mobile phone.

Rule **Connectives** are words and phrases that help to sequence ideas across a text. They can be **adverbs**, **conjunctions** or **phrases**.

firstly finally as well as alternatively although when while

1 Read *Recycle!*. Circle the **connectives**. Hint! These give the text a logical sequence.

2 How many reasons does the speaker give to support recycling mobile phones? ☐

3 Number the sentences from 1 to 5 to show the sequence. Hint! The **connectives** will help you.

☐ So, choose sandwiches for lunch today.

☐ To begin with, sandwiches are healthy.

☐ Finally, sandwiches can easily be packed for school lunches.

☐ Sandwiches are good for lunch.

☐ In addition, sandwiches are economical.

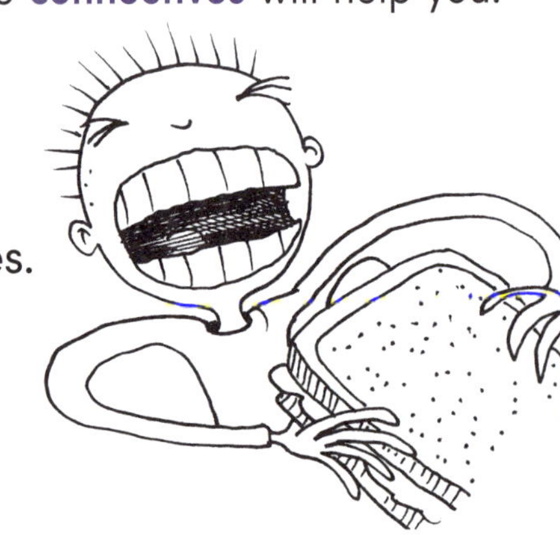

Grammar Rules! Student Book 3 (ISBN 9780655092513) © Tanya Gibb

4 Use the **connectives** from the box to complete the text below. Use a capital letter if it begins a sentence.

in addition	finally	while	secondly	firstly

I believe that television is unhealthy.

_______________, it encourages people to sit around and not exercise.

_______________, people tend to eat more _______________ they watch television.

_______________, the shows on television do not stimulate the brain.

_______________, television stops families from having conversations.

People should watch less television.

Statements can express **facts** or **opinions**. Opinions can include words that are emotive.

Fact: *Anzac biscuits are made with oats.*

Opinion: *Anzac biscuits are best when they are soft and gooey.*

5 Link each statement to FACT or OPINION.

There's a wattle tree in Aunty's yard.

Wattle trees have beautiful yellow flowers.

Pop's poodle is cute.

The whale stranding was a tragedy.

Dolphins love to help people.

FACT

OPINION

Pete's mobile phone is broken.

Whales are mammals.

Dolphins are smarter than orcas.

6 *Recycle!* ends with a call to action. Write it here.

____

Write a **speech** to **persuade** class members to do something. It could be about reducing litter, raising money for a charity, donating old toys, joining a team or anything else. Use words that are **emotive**. Use **connectives** to link your ideas logically. End with a call to action. Ask a peer to help edit your work. Rehearse your speech before presenting it to the class.

Unit 21

Quoted speech, stereotypes

This imaginative text is a comic strip **narrative**. It uses speech balloons to show what the character is saying.

PROFESSOR SNODGRASS FAILS AGAIN

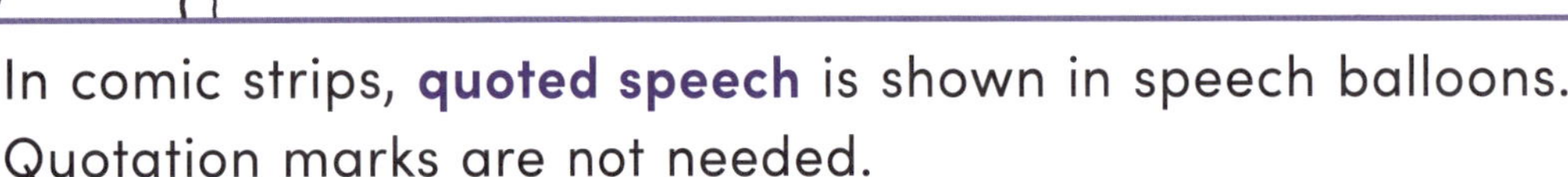

Tip In comic strips, **quoted speech** is shown in speech balloons. Quotation marks are not needed.

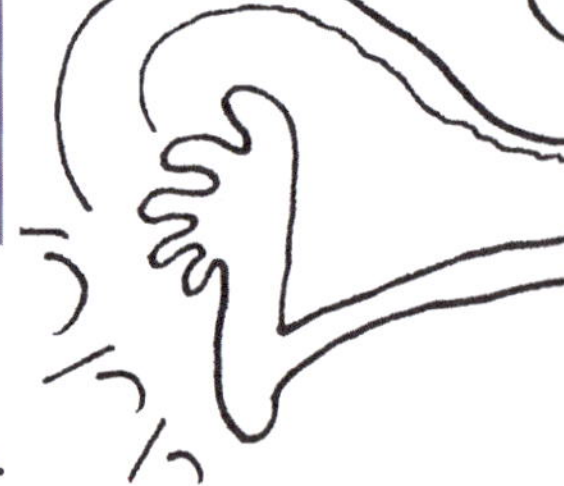

1 Read *Professor Snodgrass Fails Again.* Write what the professor says on the lines below. Use complete sentences with **quotation marks** and **saying verbs**.

____

____

____

2 What would you say to Professor Snodgrass if you met him? Write your speech using **quotation marks**.

____

____

Grammar Rules! Student Book 3 (ISBN 9780655092513) © Tanya Gibb

3 Write speech inside each speech balloon.

4 Read out loud the made-up term *'curus maximus stinkolata footitis'*. Have a guess what each word could mean.

Cartoons and comic strips often use **stereotypes**. A stereotype is a caricature or an oversimplification. The image of Professor Snodgrass is a **stereotype**, not a true-to-life image of a professor.

5 Draw a line to connect each description to either a real-life scientist or a stereotype.

works in a laboratory or in the field

male only

may or may not wear glasses or contact lenses

male or female

works in a laboratory only

real-life scientist

stereotype scientist

wears crooked, broken glasses

has no friends

does crazy experiments and always causes explosions

nutty and mad

works safely

works alone

intelligent

Create a comic strip of your own to tell a narrative. Base your comic strip on a character that you can **stereotype** (e.g. brave hero, nosy neighbour, villain). Use speech balloons for what the characters say.

Unit 22

Emotive words, synonyms, abstract nouns

This article **reports** events that have happened. It uses **emotive words** to make the events seem more interesting.

Daily News 7 August

DINOSAUR FOUND AT LOCAL SCHOOL

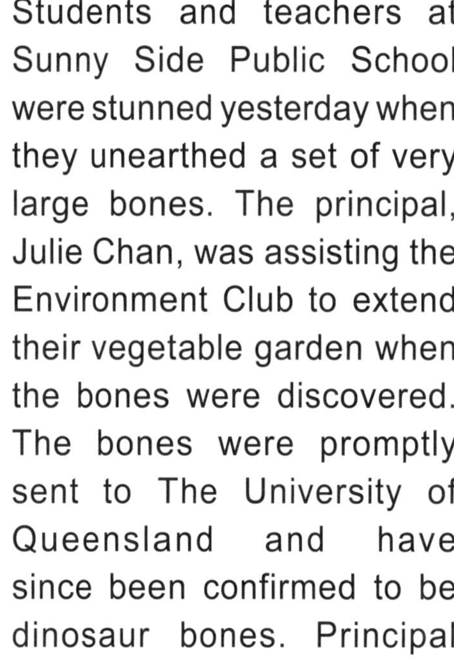

Students and teachers at Sunny Side Public School were stunned yesterday when they unearthed a set of very large bones. The principal, Julie Chan, was assisting the Environment Club to extend their vegetable garden when the bones were discovered. The bones were promptly sent to The University of Queensland and have since been confirmed to be dinosaur bones. Principal Chan said that the school community is very excited to have uncovered these incredible pieces of history.

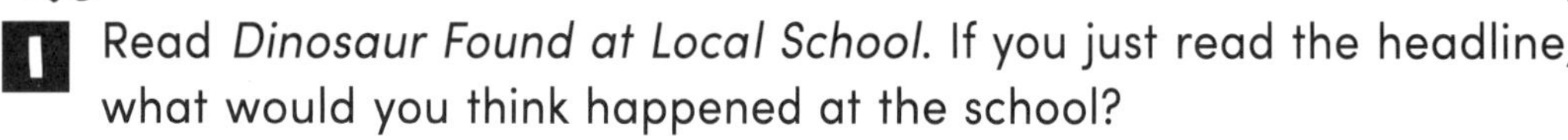

Tip News items sometimes use **emotive words** to sensationalise the writing. This creates interest.

1 Read *Dinosaur Found at Local School*. If you just read the headline, what would you think happened at the school?

____

2 What would be a more accurate but less sensational headline?

____

3 Which headline do you prefer and why?

CHILDREN DIG UP DINOSAUR

DINOSAUR IN VEGIE PATCH

DINOSAUR FOUND AT LOCAL SCHOOL

DINOSAUR DISCOVERY

____

____

Synonyms are words that have similar meanings.
beautiful/pretty *small/tiny* *coarse/rough* *clever/smart*

4 Find **synonyms** in the text for the following words.

shocked ______________ immediately ______________ uncovered ______________

helping ______________ found ______________ thrilled ______________

huge ______________ amazing ______________ expand ______________

5 Find the word in the text that means 'dug up'. ____________________

6 What are the *incredible pieces of history* in the news report?

____

7 Find and write four **adjectives** used in the news report.

____

8 Find the **adverb** that ends in *-ly* in the news report. ____________________

9 Circle the **modal verbs** in each sentence.

'There might be more bones,' suggested Ulrike.

'There must be!' declared Jon.

'We could dig for some,' offered Evan.

'We should come back after school,' said Izzy.

Which child above makes the strongest statement? ____________________

Rule

Nouns can be **abstract**. *peace hatred*
Nouns can also be **concrete**. *chair horse*

10 Find and circle the **abstract noun** *history* in *Dinosaur Found at Local School*. Underline three **concrete nouns**.

Write a news article that reports about something that has happened at your school. Use **emotive language** to make the events sound exciting. Don't forget to write an attention-grabbing headline.

Unit 23 Verbs, tense, story characters

The Discovery

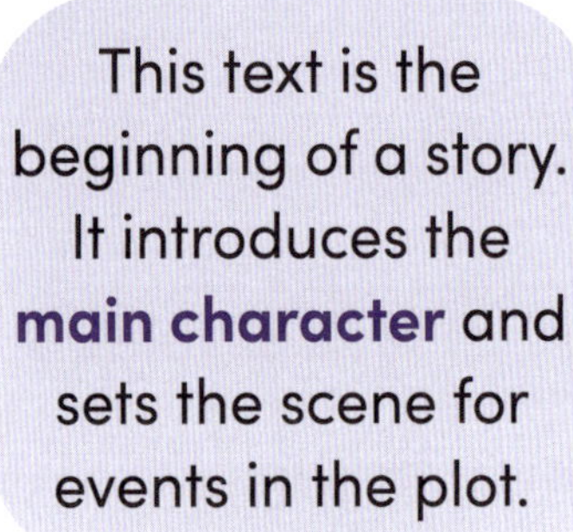

This text is the beginning of a story. It introduces the **main character** and sets the scene for events in the plot.

Ella's family was camping in the mountains. One night, after taking her little sister to their parents' tent, Ella noticed something colourful stuck in the tree branches above the camp site. It was too dark to see properly, so she decided to wait until morning to have a better look. The next morning, as soon as she woke, Ella climbed the tree to see what was hidden in the branches. It was a high climb, but eventually she reached the section of the tree that held the object. She discovered that it was a very small jacket, only big enough for a very tiny person, and there was something in the pocket.

Rule

Verbs can show when an action happened. This is called **tense**.

past tense	*She went.*	*She has gone.*
present tense	*She goes.*	*She is going.*
future tense	*She will go.*	

1 Read *The Discovery*. Underline three **prepositional phrases** that tell where.

2 **Past tense verbs** often end in *-ed*. Circle five past tense verbs in *The Discovery* that end in *-ed*.

3 Tick a column to show the **tense** of each sentence.

	Past	Present	Future
I am hungry.			
I chased the cat.			
I will go to the park.			
You are standing in the way.			
You stepped on my toes.			

4 Complete the table.

Past	Present	Future
I jumped.	I am jumping.	I will jump.
I ate.		
	I am skipping.	
I played.		
I wrote.		
		I might help.

5 Add some other **past tense verbs** to replace *got* in this paragraph.

Ella (got) ______________ down from the tree. She (got) ______________ into her tent. She (got) ______________ her sister to hold the jacket. She (got) ______________ her reading glasses from her backpack for a closer look.

6 What have your learned about Ella's character in the story so far? Circle the **adjectives** you judge to be true about her.

Ella seems:

observant timid strong cheeky interested sensible reckless

brave adventurous curious stubborn kind argumentative

Share your selections with a partner. Justify your choices.

7 Would you like Ella as a friend? Why or why not?

____

____

Write a **narrative** of your own. Use words and phrases that show the sequence of events. Use **adjectives** to describe the characters. Ask a classmate to proofread and help edit your work.

Unit 24 Revision

1 Use an apostrophe to show **possession**.

The dog belongs to Jude. It is Jude's dog.

The keys belong to Aunty. They are ________________.

The paw belongs to the cat. It is the ________________.

The children own the skateboards. They are the ________________.

The teachers own the cars. They are the ________________.

2 Number the sentences from 1 to 5 to show the sequence.

- [ ] Therefore, I recommend soccer to everyone.
- [ ] Firstly, it gives you a lot of exercise.
- [ ] My third point is that it teaches you how to be part of a team.
- [ ] I think soccer is a great sport.
- [ ] Secondly, it teaches you lots of skills.

3 Write two **facts** and two **opinions** about your class.

Fact	Opinion
________________	________________
________________	________________
________________	________________

4 Add **quotation marks** to show **quoted speech**.

Your dad was as fast as lightning when he was your age, said Nonna.

Dad said, Not anymore.

Why not? I asked.

My knee is kaput, replied Dad, sadly.

What's kaput? I asked and Nonna raised her eyebrows.

Guess! said Dad.

Grammar Rules! Student Book 3 (ISBN 9780655092513) © Tanya Gibb

5 Imagine that your school principal won the lottery and decided to take the whole school on a holiday to Fiji. Write a newspaper headline about it. Use **emotive words**.

____

6 Find synonyms in this text for the words below.

> It's exciting to watch Madison de Rozario compete in wheelchair racing. She is an amazing athlete. Racing wheelchairs have two large wheels at the back and one smaller wheel at the front. Racers need powerful upper bodies to reach speeds of more than 30kmph. It can be dangerous.

strong ______________ competitors ______________ risky ______________

thrilling ______________ incredible ______________ big ______________

7 Tick a column to show the tense of each sentence.

	Past	Present	Future
I am tired.			
I fed the hippos.			
Will we go to the park?			
You are blocking the doorway.			
You squashed the banana.			
We might go to the movies on Saturday.			

8 Cross out the incorrect **verb**.

I (go/went) to the shop yesterday.

I (bought/will buy) a milkshake later.

Mary (played/plays) cricket last Saturday.

Rami (rid/rode) his bike to school this morning.

9 Number these sentences from 1 to 4 in time order.

☐ After school, we had gymnastics.

☐ Before lunch, we marked our homework.

☐ After lunch, we had art.

☐ Before school, I went to the library.

Unit **25** Modal verbs and adverbs, conjunctions

This **persuasive** text summarises different points of view. It uses the **conjunction** *because* to link opinions with reasons.

THE BEST NEW INVENTION

A number of amazing inventions have been entered in the Best New Invention Competition.

Many people think the Heli Cooler Hat should win because it keeps people cool on a hot day. The 40-centimetre blades are attached to the top of a sunhat. When the 'on' switch is pressed, the blades whirl around like a fan.

Other people prefer the Santa Claus Detector because it sets off a silent alarm the second Santa Claus falls down the chimney.

Every young child will want a Santa Claus Detector, for sure. However, my vote goes to the Heli Cooler Hat because I think it will be useful every day and it is also great for keeping people sun safe.

1 Read *The Best New Invention*. Underline the **noun group** at the beginning of each paragraph.

2 Draw a line to link each paragraph in *The Best New Invention* with its purpose.

Paragraph 1	to present an opinion and give reasons
Paragraph 2	to make a final recommendation or judgement
Paragraph 3	to present a different opinion and give reasons
Paragraph 4	to introduce the topic

Rule

Conjunctions and other connecting words can link an opinion with a reason or condition.

because although so however since unless in case otherwise

3 Circle the **conjunction** in *The Best New Invention* that links each opinion with a reason.

Grammar Rules! Student Book 3 (ISBN 9780655092513) © Tanya Gibb

4 Choose a **conjunction** from the box to join the clauses correctly.

although	because	otherwise	so	unless

I like apples better than oranges ______________ they are sweeter.

I'll have the orange ______________ I prefer apples.

You don't like apples ______________ take an orange in your lunch box.

I don't like apples ______________ they are very crisp.

You should eat them before they go bad ______________ they'll be wasted.

Different **modal verbs** and **adverbs** are used for different **audiences** and **purposes**. In an advertisement, it is important to express certainty.

This is definitely the very best product on the market. You must buy it!

When interacting with others, it is important to respond respectfully.

You made some good points but perhaps we could try something else.

5 Draw a line to link each comment to the person most likely to say it.

I see what you mean but I'm not sure I agree.

You are absolutely wrong.

I understand what you're saying.

That's a good point but I can't agree.

Maybe you have a point.

That is a stupid suggestion.

Your opinion is ridiculous.

You can't be serious.

I'm not sure I can agree with what you've said.

We should probably think about these ideas a little more.

Thank you for your ideas but I disagree.

disrespectful

respectful

Discuss your favourite gadget or invention with a partner. Listen and comment respectfully. Use words such as *I think, possibly, perhaps*. Record the opinions presented and the reasons for them in a written **discussion**. Use the same structure as in *The Best New Invention*.

Unit 26 Prefixes, suffixes, describing and number adjectives

This report is **informative**. It provides factual information about the topic. It uses topic-specific terminology.

Creation Stories

Creation stories are stories that have been told from one First Nations generation to the next for thousands of years. Creation stories teach important lessons about sharing resources, caring for Country and valuing the knowledge of Elders.

The story of a water-holding frog, who greedily drinks all the water in the land, is a creation story of the Gunaikurnai people, as well as other Australian First Nations groups. In some of the stories about the water-guzzling frog, when the frog laughs, the land floods and many creatures drown.

The story of Tiddalick, the greedy frog, is based on a First Nations story.

1 Read *Creation Stories*. Complete the sentence.

Some creation stories do not have a happy ending because ______________________

____

2 In *Creation Stories*, find and underline four **noun groups** that refer to the frog.

3 Write the **adverb** in *Creation Stories* that tells how the frog drank. ______________________

4 Add a **conjunction** to connect the clauses.

First Nations stories are important ______________________ they explain people's connection to Country, plants and animals.

5 Rewrite the sentences with correct punctuation.

the giant frog is molok in some parts of australia said harriet

____

different first nations peoples have different creation stories said kaya

____

Grammar Rules! Student Book 3 (ISBN 9780655092513) © Tanya Gibb

Prefixes are letters or word parts added to the front of words. **Suffixes** are added to the ends of words. They form plurals and show tense. Prefixes and suffixes change word meanings.

happy–unhappy *understood–misunderstood* *care–careful–careless*

6 Add a **prefix** from the box to each word. You can use any prefix twice.

un	im	il	re	in	non	ir

do ______________ send ______________

correct ______________ sense ______________

logical ______________ like ______________

important ______________________

7 Draw a line to match each describing **adjective** with a **noun**.

endangered	melody
prickly	aunt
colourful	forest
dense	lorikeet
tuneful	cactus
thoughtful	numbat

Rule

A **noun group** can include **adjectives** that show possession, describe and tell number, order or quantity.

his last apple *a few goannas* *their first home* *one wise old owl*

8 Underline all the **adjectives** in the sentences.

'I know a few words in the Gubbi Gubbi language,' declared Rami.

'I know twenty Gubbi Gubbi words,' said Lane, 'including "Wunya Ngulumi!"'

'I speak some Gubbi Gubbi. My knowledge is better than yours,' said Indya.

9 Complete the paragraph using **adjectives** from the box.

black	bottom	red	top	yellow	two

The Australian Aboriginal Flag is a rectangle divided into ______________ halves. The ______________ half is ______________ for the people. The ______________ half is ______________ for the earth. The flag has a ______________ sun in the centre.

Find a First Nations creation story that you like. Work in a group. Plan how to **retell** or act out the story for the rest of the class. Present the story. Summarise the lesson or moral at the end of your presentation.

This is a **recipe**. Its title tells the goal. It includes a list of ingredients. The method lists steps to follow in sequence.

Wart, Fester and Carbuncle Remover

Ingredients

- 1 cup milk
- 100 g grated candle wax
- 1 tablespoon very hot chilli powder
- 10 ml nail polish remover
- 2 cups vinegar

What is a carbuncle, anyway?

Method

1. Mix all ingredients into a paste.
2. Apply a thin film of paste over affected areas.
3. Bandage affected areas.
4. Avoid water for four weeks. (This means no baths or showers.)

1 Read *Wart, Fester and Carbuncle Remover*. Circle the **adjectives** that tell the amount of each ingredient to use.

2 What do *g* and *ml* mean in the recipe? ______________ ______________

3 Complete each sentence with a word from the box. Make sure each sentence makes sense.

enough a pinch 200 g 1 litre

Add ______________ of salt.

Add ______________ water to make a smooth paste.

Add ______________ of sugar.

Stir in ______________ of milk.

4 Use a dictionary. Write the definition of *carbuncle*.

____

Write the definition of *fester* as it is used in the text.

____

What is a wart?

____

Grammar Rules! Student Book 3 (ISBN 9780655092513) © Tanya Gibb

5 Underline the **number adjectives**.

The third runner is my friend.

A few friends are coming.

I won second prize for my invention.

I have three cats.

Many schools organise excursions to the museum.

A hundred people went to the concert.

Tip

The method of a recipe is a series of **commands**. Most commands start with a **doing verb**.
Sometimes commands start with an **adverb** that tells how to do something.

6 Write the **doing verbs** in *Wart, Fester and Carbuncle Remover.*

__________ __________ __________ __________

7 Use an **adverb** from the box to start each **command**.

carefully	briskly	gently	totally

1. __________ mix all ingredients into a paste.
2. __________ apply a thin film of paste over affected areas.
3. __________ bandage affected areas.
4. __________ avoid water for four weeks.

8 Would you use the recipe *Warts, Festers and Carbuncle Remover* if you had a wart? Explain.

____

____

____

Try it yourself!

Create a **recipe** to cure a real sickness or a made-up sickness, such as school fever or breatho stinko o'lot'o. Use **number adjectives** for the amounts of each ingredient. Use a **doing verb** or **adverb** at the beginning of each **command**.

Unit 28

Conjunctions, adverbs, verb groups

This is an **explanation**. An explanation tells how or why something happens. Information is sequenced in time or through cause and effect.

How the Alarm Bed Works

1. An alarm clock, attached to the head of the bed, rings when it is time for the sleeper to get up.
2. When it rings, the sleeper has five minutes to get out of bed because that alarm starts a five-minute timer in the mattress springs.
3. If the pressure on the mattress springs has not changed when the five minutes are up (in other words, if the sleeper is still in the bed), then a latch at the head of the bed is released. This causes the mattress and bed base to catapult upward.
4. Then the sleeper is ejected from the bed.

1 What changes the pressure on the mattress springs?

____

Circle the correct movement of the bed.

When the bed base catapults upward it a) glides on springs b) moves suddenly and quickly or c) rises off the floor.

Conjunctions and **adverbs** connect ideas in time or through cause and effect.

then *next* *when* *until* *therefore* *however* *if*

2 Find and circle the words that sequence events in *How the Alarm Bed Works.*

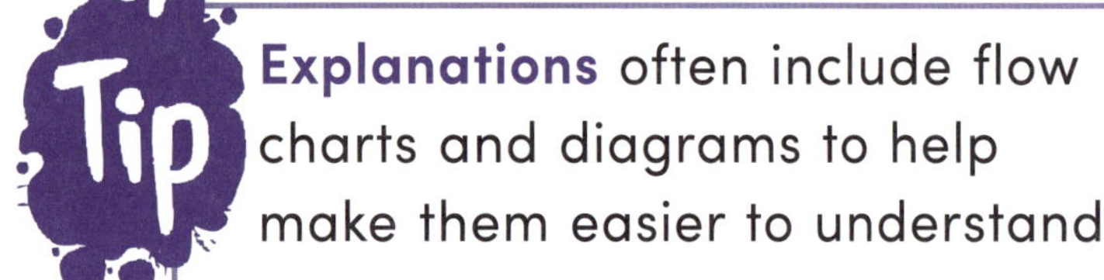

Explanations often include flow charts and diagrams to help make them easier to understand.

3 On spare paper, draw an illustration to match one of the steps in *How the Alarm Bed Works.* Share and discuss your illustration with a partner.

4 Write a list of things you would need to construct the alarm bed. These things will be **nouns**.

____

____

____

Grammar Rules! Student Book 3 (ISBN 9780655092513) © Tanya Gibb

5 Choose a **conjunction** from the box to join the clauses.

BOING

because
then
so
Unless
until

Sleep soundly __________ the alarm goes off.

The alarm bed is effective __________ it gets you out of bed.

__________ you get up within five minutes, the bed will eject you.

Don't go back to sleep __________ the bed base will catapult upward.

Being ejected from bed is not fun __________ don't try to sleep in.

6 Write the **doing verb** for each step in the process.

a. The alarm clock ______________.

b. The alarm clock ______________ a timer.

c. The latch ______________.

d. The mattress and bed base ______________.

e. The sleeper is ______________.

Rule

A **verb group** is a group of words that includes a verb. A verb group might include a **helping verb** (e.g. *is, was, had*), a **modal verb** (e.g. *can, might, should*) or an **adverb** (e.g. *quickly*).

had been baking   *is going*   *has eaten*   *will follow*   *mustn't go*   *gently touched*

7 Circle the **verb** or **verb group** in each clause.

Anders had been sleeping when the bed ejected him.

Leo was catapulted from his bed this morning.

Evey didn't stay in bed when her alarm started ringing.

Remy might set his alarm bed for 7 o'clock tomorrow.

8 Use **evaluative words** to write your opinion of the alarm bed and your reasons. Is it useful? Will it work? Will people buy it and use it?

____

____

Try it yourself!

Create an invention of your own. Then write an explanation to tell how it works. Use **connectives** to show time and to show cause and effect. Or, imagine your new alarm bed ejected you early one very cold winter morning. Write your response.

Unit 29

Noun groups, sentences, clauses

How to Use the Drolley (or Dog Trolley)

The Drolley (Dog Trolley) allows you to walk a number of dogs at the same time.

1. Attach each dog's lead to a special hook on the Drolley and then push the Drolley to walk the dogs. A brake in the hook activates automatically if any dog pulls too hard.
2. Use the Drolley's plastic suction hose to suck up dog droppings, so they can be treated with environmentally-safe chemicals and then used to fertilise your garden.
3. Store drinking bowls and dog treats in the Drolley's tray, which is located along the side of the Drolley.

This **informative** text tells the purpose of a device and how to use it. The instructions use **commands** and **doing verbs**.

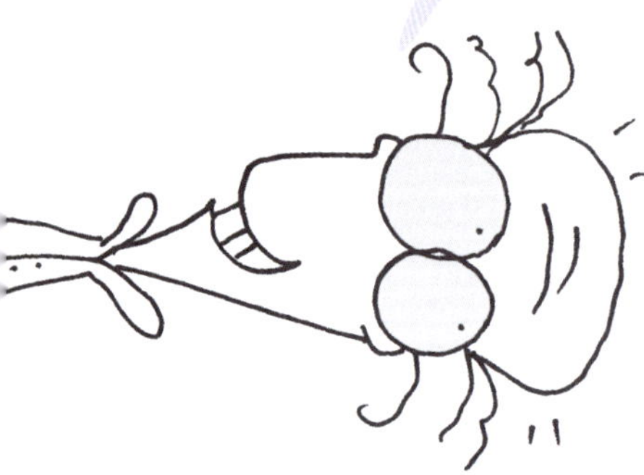

1 Read *How to Use the Drolley (or Dog Trolley)*. Underline four **clauses** that are **commands**. Hint! Remember that every clause has a **verb** or **verb group**.

Sometimes nouns are used as **adjectives** to classify in a noun group.

timber floor *basketball match* *ballet shoes* *coconut biscuits*

2 Underline the **noun groups**. Circle the **adjectives** that classify.

Use the treated dog droppings as fertiliser.

Dog treats can be stored in the tray.

It has a plastic suction hose.

That dog has a leather collar.

It makes an unusual garden fertiliser.

Elkie wore a straw sunhat on her walk.

The rubber wheels made it easy to steer.

3 Choose a **noun** from the box to classify each noun below.

rain	oak	fruit	tin	chocolate	refrigerator
hand	marsupial	money	football		

_______________ tree _______________ shed _______________ truck

_______________ cloud _______________ box _______________ cake

_______________ boot _______________ juice _______________ bag

_______________ mouse

4 Add a **noun group** to each line to complete the sentence.
For example: *A person who teaches is a teacher.*

A person who invents is _______________________.

A person who performs magic tricks is _______________________.

A person who studies is _______________________.

A person who plays a musical instrument is _______________________.

A person who acts is _______________________.

A person who conducts an orchestra is _______________________.

A person who plays the piano is _______________________.

A person who works in the field of science is _______________________.

5 Add a **clause** to complete each sentence.

The Drolley works best when ____

The Drolley topples over if ____

The Drolley's wheels freeze up when ____

The treated dog business is released when ____

Write a **procedure** (instructions) for using a piece of equipment. Or, invent something, describe its features and write instructions for how to use it.

Unit

30 Revision

1 Complete each sentence with a **connective** from the box. Use a capital letter if the connective begins a sentence.

so	since	unless	in case	otherwise

____________ we can't have cake, let's have ice cream.

Take your raincoat ____________ it starts to rain.

Start your homework straight away. ____________ you won't finish before dinner.

____________ you start now you won't be finished before dinner.

Get your homework finished ____________ you can watch some television.

2 Circle the **connective** in each sentence and then underline the **clauses**.

Harlow is feeling healthier because she is eating more vegetables.

Noah offered to help if his help was needed.

Rimma has a walking frame so Hussein walks slowly with her.

Liam has become more outgoing since he made friends with Peter.

Naseem and Usman are good friends but they don't enjoy the same novels.

3 Replace the **adjectives** in brackets with more interesting adjectives.

We saw a (great) ______________ band called 'King Stingray' at a concert the other night. I loved their songs. They sing in Yolngu and English. They are (great) ______________ musicians.

I saw their music video 'Camp dog'. It was (great) ______________.

4 Add one or more **clauses** to each sentence.

Bells work ____

____

Dog leashes work ___________________________________

____

Grammar Rules! Student Book 3 (ISBN 9780655092513) © Tanya Gibb

5 Complete each sentence with a **number adjective** from the box.

Some
Many
2
one
few

Buy __________ litres of milk, please.

__________ people attended the concert.

__________ ducks swam on the lake.

A __________ houses were damaged in the storm.

Swallow __________ teaspoon of medicine.

6 Underline the **noun groups**.

Our school won first prize in the music competition.

The town debating team won a few medals.

Most school excursions are enjoyable.

Thousands of people went to the music festival.

7 Choose an **adverb** to begin each command.

Carefully
Gently
Clearly
Slowly

______________ explain your invention.

______________ stir the mixture while it heats.

______________ collect the eggs.

______________ pat the puppies.

8 Create **noun groups**. Add a word from each row to each noun below.

exciting healthy cute fresh ferocious

boxer male football orange breakfast

______________ ______________ game

______________ ______________ tiger

______________ ______________ puppy

______________ ______________ juice

______________ ______________ cereal

Collective nouns, pronouns, point of view

This poem is a **response**. It presents a point of view.

My Home

This land is mine.
The land does not belong to you.
White man is here now.
You need to understand.
We own everything.
You've caused problems:
fighting us,
killing our livestock,
burning our crops.
We've cleared the land
for our farms.
We've built houses
where there was nothing but scrub.
We've built fences
for our sheep.
'WE own this land.
There is no place for you.'

1 Read *My Home.* Who do you think is telling the story in the poem?

____

2 What is the **main idea** in the poem?

____

3 Circle all the **pronouns** in the poem.

Who is *we, us, I?* ________________________________

Who is *you?* ____________________________________

4 Underline the **verbs** in the poem.

5 What does this line tell you about the narrator's values? *where there was nothing but scrub.*

____

6 What might *You* in the poem want to say to the person telling the story in the poem?

____

Collective nouns are names for groups of things. *bunch flock gang herd*
Collective nouns are singular.
The flock has settled for the night.

7 Use a **collective noun** from the box to complete each **noun group**.

pod	team
litter	herd
flock	school

a ____________ of kittens
a ____________ of whales
a ____________ of players
a ____________ of cows
a ____________ of ducks
a ____________ of fish

8 Circle the correct **verb** or **verb group** in each row.

The herd (is travelling / are travelling) north.

The horses (are galloping / is galloping).

The pack of dingoes (are monitored / is monitored) by rangers.

The dingoes (are / is) hungry.

My mob (are heading / is heading) to town.

9 Write a **personal pronoun** on each line to complete the sentences.

That seat is not yours. ____________ do not own ____________.

We live on Country. ____________ will look after ____________.

Listen to ____________. I will tell ____________ about Country.

The wild animals belong here. ____________ need to be protected.

Think about people in history who have had different **points of view**. Write a **poem** that shows the differences. Or, write a **poem** that shows one or more points of view about an issue in your home, community or school.

Unit 32

Types of sentences, point of view, antonyms

This text shows different **points of view**. It includes a variety of sentence types.

Can We Negotiate?

'Pack up all your equipment, now,' requested Mum.

'Why can't we work on our project a bit longer?' whined Billy.

'I need the table for my work. Your experiment will have to wait until tomorrow,' insisted Mum.

'But Mum,' added Aggie, 'we just got everything organised. Can we just have another half an hour, PLEASE?'

'No! There's no time. I think it's a great project but it can wait. Finish it tomorrow,' declared Mum.

1 Read *Can We Negotiate?* Highlight what Billy says in blue. Highlight what Mum says in red. Choose a different colour and highlight what Aggie says.

2 Circle the **saying verbs** in *Can We Negotiate?*.

3 Why do you think Mum is smiling in the illustration?

____

4 Choose one **command** from *Can We Negotiate?*. Write it on the line.

____

5 What does *negotiate* mean? Write a definition. Use a dictionary.

____

6 What idea do the three people agree on in *Can We Negotiate?*

____

Grammar Rules! Student Book 3 (ISBN 9780655092513) © Tanya Gibb

7 Write a sentence of your own on each line. Use correct punctuation marks.

Statement ______________________________

Question ______________________________

Command ______________________________

Exclamation ______________________________

8 Rewrite each sentence with correct punctuation.

thats unnecessary exclaimed reema ______________________________

where is my hat questioned karl ______________________________

i love lasagne stated fema ______________________________

stop shouted the coach ______________________________

Rule

Antonyms are words that have opposite meanings. Antonyms can often be formed using **prefixes** or **suffixes**.

difficult/easy *regular/irregular* *hopeful/hopeless*

9 Write four **antonyms** for *great* as it is used in *Can We Negotiate?*.

____

10 Write three **synonyms** that could be used instead of *whined* in *Can We Negotiate?*.

____

11 Write three **synonyms** that could be used instead of *declared* in *Can We Negotiate?*.

____

12 Sometimes the word *said* is used too often in texts. This can make the text sound boring. What other words could you use in your writing instead of *said*? Start a list of **synonyms** here.

____

Write a **discussion** between two or three people. Show that they have different opinions. Use punctuation marks and include statements, questions, commands and exclamations.

Unit 33

Pronouns, modal verbs and adverbs, abstract nouns

This text is **informative**. It uses dot points and subheadings.

Clever Inventions

First Nations Australians are clever inventors. Two of their cleverest inventions are:

- **Boomerangs**

Boomerangs were invented thousands of years ago. They were used for hunting and killing animals, in warfare or as digging sticks to dig vegetables from the ground. A boomerang could kill a kangaroo or emu 60m away from a thrower. Most boomerangs were non-returning. This clever invention is an important symbol of Australia.

- **Cultural burning**

Cultural burning is a method of controlled burning that First Nations Australians have used for thousands of years. Controlled burning is used to clear vegetation to make hunting easier, to encourage new plant growth and to prevent wildfires.

1 Read *Clever Inventions*. List three uses for a boomerang.

______

______

______

2 What opinion does the writer of *Clever Inventions* have about boomerangs?

______

3 List three reasons for cultural burning.

______

______

______

Grammar Rules! Student Book 3 (ISBN 9780655092513) © Tanya Gibb

4 Find and circle the **noun group** *This clever invention* in *Clever Inventions*.

What is *This clever invention?* ____________________

5 Circle the **modal verb** in the sentence that tells you that the result was not certain.

A boomerang could kill a kangaroo or emu 60m away from a thrower.

6 Write a **personal pronoun** on each line.

Boomerangs were invented thousands of years ago. ________ were used for hunting.

The boomerang is a symbol of Australia. ________ is recognised internationally.

Cultural burning is a controlled burning. First Nations Australians have practised ________ for thousands of years.

7 Write two **abstract nouns** used in *Clever Inventions*.

____________________ ____________________

Tip Remember the rule on page 51.

8 Tick the **sentence** that expresses the most certainty.

- [ ] Cultural burning might not prevent wildfires.
- [ ] Cultural burning will prevent wildfires.
- [ ] Cultural burning could help to prevent wildfires.

9 Rewrite the sentence using correct **punctuation**.

boomerangs were invented in australia declared zali

____

did you know that there are paintings of boomerangs on 20 000 year old rock art asked kyra

____

____

Research an Australian First Nations invention, such as the woomera, the didgeridoo or the waterbag. Create a **report** to present your research to your class or another group.

Unit 34

Personal pronouns, commas in lists, homophones

This **information report** uses **personal pronouns** to refer to people and things and to make the text **cohesive.**

The Invention of Money

It is thought that the Greeks invented the first money over two and a half thousand years ago. They made coins out of a mixture of gold and silver.

Before the invention of money, people traded items of value. For example, a farmer might trade a cow for two pigs. Other items that people traded were rice, tobacco, animal furs, whale teeth and gold.

Gold was a popular trading item, but it was too heavy to carry around, so people wrote promises on pieces of paper saying they would pay in gold. The first true paper money was probably invented in China.

1 List the items people traded before the invention of money.

____

2 Circle a **sentence** in *The Invention of Money* that tells you the writer is not certain of the facts.

3 Find a **personal pronoun** in *The Invention of Money*. ______________

Who or what does the **pronoun** refer to? ______________

4 Write five **noun groups** used in *The Invention of Money*.

____

Remember the rule on page 59.

5 Write two **proper nouns** for people or countries used in *The Invention of Money*.

____

6 What was the advantage of paper money?

____

Grammar Rules! Student Book 3 (ISBN 9780655092513) © Tanya Gibb

Commas are used to separate items in a list of **nouns**. The word *and* is usually used instead of a comma between the last two items.

rice, tobacco, animal furs, whale teeth and gold

7 Write lists. Use **commas** between each item and the word *and* between the last two items.

girls' names ____________, ____________, ____________ and ____________

boys' names ____

friends' names ____

items you could trade ____

____

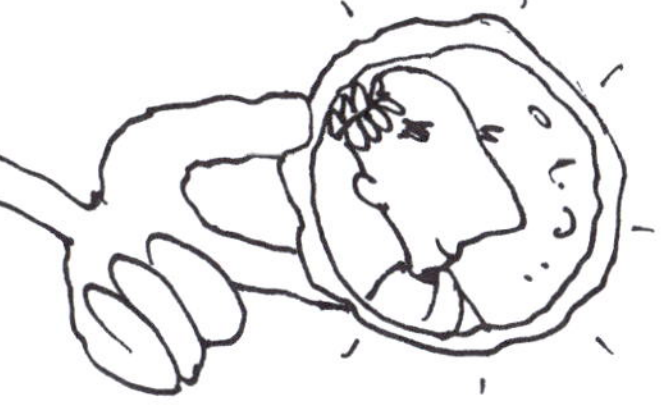

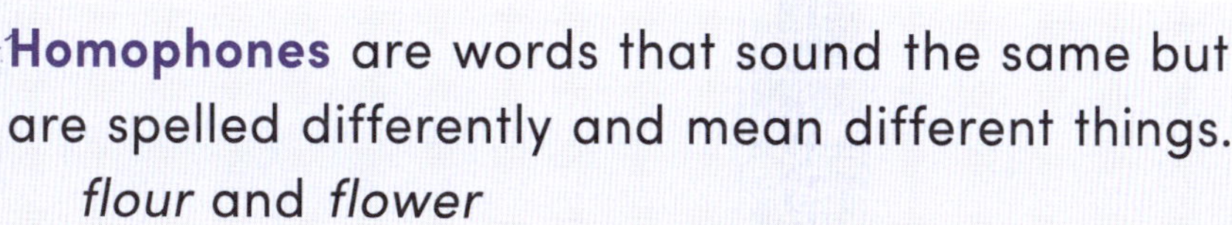

Homophones are words that sound the same but are spelled differently and mean different things.

flour and *flower*

8 Find a **homophone** for *two* and *to* in *The Invention of Money*. ____________

9 Circle the correct **homophone** in each sentence.

The (sail / sale) of the boat fluttered in the breeze.

The (weather / whether) was very mild.

(There / Their) sailboat was very slow.

(Buy / By) the time the wind picked up, we had to go home.

I ran out of (flour / flower) to make the cake.

Do some research on a topic of your choice. Write an **information report**. Use **personal pronouns** to refer to people or things you are writing about. Be careful not to give your opinions. Only write the facts.

Unit 35 Revision

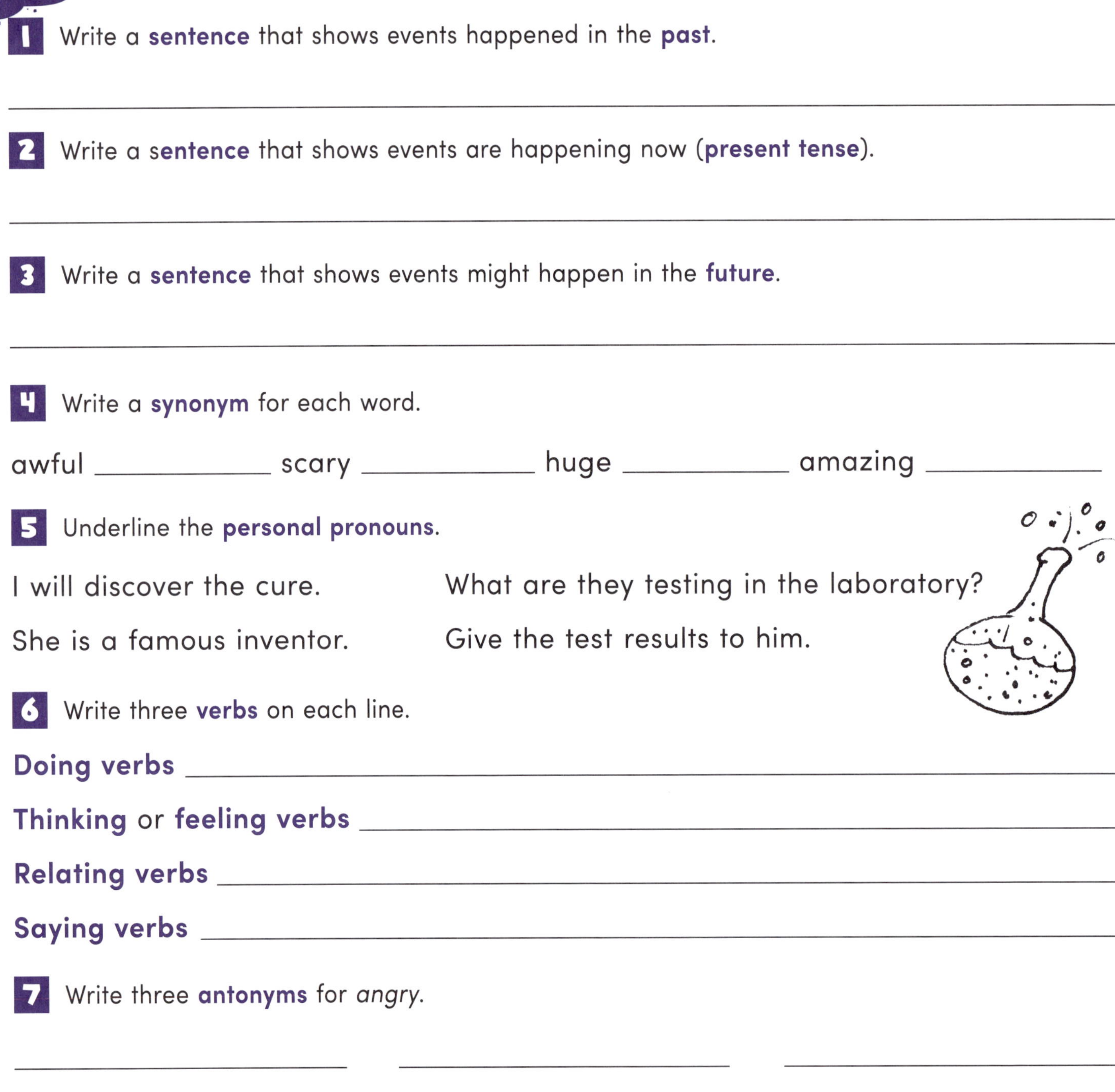

1 Write a **sentence** that shows events happened in the **past**.

____

2 Write a **sentence** that shows events are happening now (**present tense**).

____

3 Write a **sentence** that shows events might happen in the **future**.

____

4 Write a **synonym** for each word.

awful ____________ scary ____________ huge ____________ amazing ____________

5 Underline the **personal pronouns**.

I will discover the cure.

She is a famous inventor.

What are they testing in the laboratory?

Give the test results to him.

6 Write three **verbs** on each line.

Doing verbs ____

Thinking or **feeling verbs** ____

Relating verbs ____

Saying verbs ____

7 Write three **antonyms** for *angry*.

____________ ____________ ____________

8 Underline each statement that presents an opinion.

My cousin is greedy.

That's a funny movie.

The strawberries are expensive.

Chantel has black hair.

9 Add **commas** to this sentence.

We will need a hammer some nails a piece of paper a pen and our thinking caps!

Grammar Rules! Student Book 3 (ISBN 9780655092513) © Tanya Gibb

10 Add punctuation to these sentences.

thats my hat shouted raphael

does anyone have the football asked Jordan

come here commanded the teacher

we need to finish our group project today reminded Sunita

11 Add **adjectives** to build interesting **noun groups** for a spooky story.

____________ ____________ wolf ____________ ____________ castle

____________ ____________ forest ____________ ____________ goblin

12 Circle the correct **verb** or **verb group** in each row.

Mum (goes / go) to work by bus.

The herd of elephants (are / is) wary.

The team (are heading / is heading) to the oval.

Those dingoes (are / is) hungry.

13 Add a **prefix** to each word to create **antonyms**.

understood ________________ responsible ________________

logical ________________ ability ________________

14 Add a **conjunction** from the box to each sentence to join the clauses. Use a capital letter if the conjunction begins a sentence.

although	unless	so	after

Jasmine was scared of the dark ______________ she made her sister walk with her.

Lloyd couldn't watch television ______________ his homework was completed.

______________ his homework was completed, Lloyd watched television.

______________ Nikita wanted to watch her show, she let Gabby watch the news.

15 Circle the **abstract nouns**.

footpath idea concrete heavy lonely cleanliness

peace education history pride handshake computer

Glossary

Look at the page number in the circle to find more information about the rule or tip.

adjective............a word that tells more about a **noun** 10

to classify 64

to compare or show preference 41

to describe 10 15

to show possession 59

to tell number or quantity 15 59

adverb................a word that can tell 25

where 29 *how* 29

when/time 25 *modal adverbs* 35

antonym............a word that means the opposite of another word 71

apostrophe.......a punctuation mark; used in a **contraction** 23

used to show possession 23

article ....*(a, an, the)* used in front of a **noun** or at the beginning of a **noun group** 15

body language...........gestures and facial expressions used for effect and to influence listeners or viewers 34

clause.................a unit of meaning that includes a **verb** 11

comma...............a punctuation mark that separates items in a series 37

lists 75 *used in quoted speech* 37

command..........a sentence that tells someone to do something 39

compound sentence............a sentence consisting of two independent clauses joined by a coordinating conjunction 26

conjunction.......a type of connecting word that joins **clauses** in sentences 26 56

connective........a word or words that link ideas through a text 46

contraction.......a word made by shortening words and leaving letters out 23

emotive words.words chosen to make readers or listeners feel a certain way 38 50

evaluative word...................words that tell us someone's opinion and judgement about something 33

exclamation......a word or sentence that shows strong emotion, or gives a warning or command; ends in an exclamation mark 28

fact.....................something that is usually accepted as true 47

homophone.......a word that sounds the same as another word but is spelled differently and means something different 75

idiom..................an expression that means something different from the words used 45

imagery.............words that help create a picture in the mind or that appeal to the senses 44

Grammar Rules! Student Book 3 (ISBN 9780655092513) © Tanya Gibb

independent clause.................a simple sentence; a clause that makes sense on its own 11

main idea..........the idea the writer or speaker wants you to know or accept as true 22

noun...................a naming word for people, places, animals and things, including ideas

classifying 64 *collective* 69
common or proper 8 *concrete or abstract* 51
noun group 15 59 *singular and plural* 27

onomatopoeia..when a word imitates a sound 29

opinion..............a statement that reveals what the speaker or writer thinks 47

personal pronoun............a word that refers to or replaces a **noun** 12

possessive pronoun............a pronoun that shows possession 36

prefix.................letters or a word part added to the beginning of a word 59

prepositional phrase (adverbial)...............a group of words not including a verb and beginning with a preposition; can tell when 20

question...........a sentence that asks for information or an opinion. It ends in a question mark. 24

quoted speech..the actual speech someone says; uses quotation marks 32

sentence...........a group of words that makes sense on its own and includes at least one verb 11

a simple sentence is one clause (includes one verb/verb group) 11
a compound sentence contains two independent clauses joined by a coordinating conjunction 26

simile.................when something is said to be like or as something else 45

statements........a sentence that gives information or an opinion 24 47

stereotype.........a caricature or oversimplification of a person or thing 49

subject-verb agreement........the way the form of the verb changes to agree with its subject in number 27

suffix.................letters added to the end of words for plurals or to change word meanings 59

synonym...........a word that has a similar meaning to another word 51

tense.................how the form of the **verb** changes to anchor events in time 9 52

verb....................a word that tells what is happening in a clause

doing 9 *modal* 35 57 *relating (being)* 25 *saying* 16
tense 9 52 *thinking and feeling* 13 *verb group* 63

voice..................the volume, pace and tone of speech used for effect 34

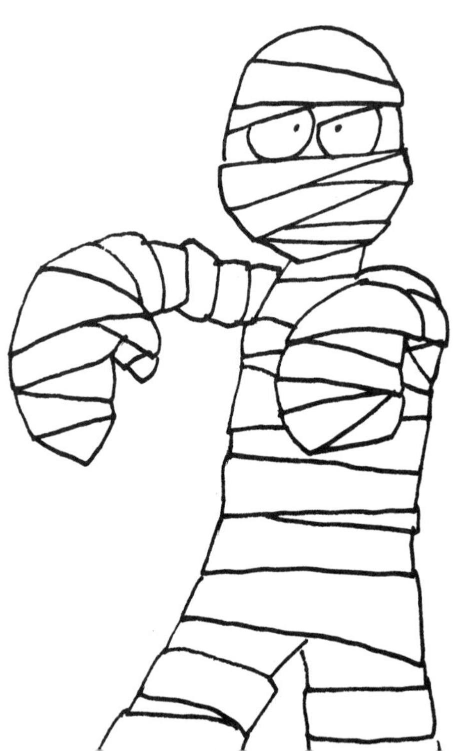